Living Architecture
FRANK LLOYD WRIGHT

Britannica Bookshelf—Great Lives for Young Americans

Living Architecture

Frank Lloyd Wright

by *Doris Ransohoff*

Published by
BRITANNICA BOOKS
a division of
ENCYCLOPAEDIA BRITANNICA, INC., Chicago

Permission to quote from the writings of Frank Lloyd Wright has been granted by the Frank Lloyd Wright Foundation, including the following works: An Autobiography (Duell, Sloane and Pearce [1943]); "The Art and Craft of the Machine," first published entire in Writings and Buildings, and other passages selected by Edgar Kaufmann and Ben Raeburn (Horizon Press, [1960]); Modern Architecture (Princeton University Press, 1931); Architecture and Modern Life (Harper's, 1937); Organic Architecture, the Architecture of Democracy (Transatlantic Arts, 1941). Permission has also been granted for use of quotations in the text and captions from Architectural Forum, Architectural Record, House Beautiful, The Spectator, the New York Times Magazine, and Reynolds Metal Company. Permission has been granted for quotation from Louis Henri Sullivan's Autobiography of an Idea (Dover Publications, Inc., 1956) and an article in Architectural Record.

For
LISA

TABLE OF CONTENTS

Part One:

The City and the Prairie

Chapter 1

The Journey Begins

U p ahead, the locomotive whistled long and plaintively, steam billowing in its wake as the curve approached. By now, they were well out of town and skimming along in the open Wisconsin countryside. Rolling hills and fields showed the fresh new green of early spring. Once in a while they passed a lazily turning windmill, a farmhouse with a cluster of outbuildings looking like toys nestled in the valley.

Frank Lloyd Wright knew the landscape by heart and loved it. But he studied it again, as though seeing it for the first time. Or, he thought to himself with a mingled thrill and sadness, as though, at 18, he were seeing it for the last time. This might very well be the case; now, at last, he was quite decisively leaving it behind.

They were running almost due south now, passing a pasture where cows grazed, amiably swishing their tails, noses buried deep in the lush grass. The sight of this rich meadow with the lazy cows taking their fill of it suddenly told him for sure that he was not only leaving the country behind. He was leaving his boyhood, too.

"Come, my boy, the cows."

In his imagination he could hear the stern voice of his Uncle James. He had been sent for the summer to the farm of his mother's family, the Lloyd-Joneses, in the Valley.

"Going to make a farmer of you my boy!" his Uncle Enos had said, and his mother had wept as her "baby's" golden curls were clipped. He must have been ten, possibly eleven, that first summer at his uncles' farm.

Even from this great distance in time, he thought he could hear the cowbells tinkling, calling to him that it was time for the cows to be fetched, rounded up wherever they might have strayed, and herded across fields and through woods to the barn for the evening milking. Left to his own devices, he would have preferred to lie dreaming in the barn loft, or to be off in the fields hunting for flame-red lilies or in the woods for lady's-slippers. His uncle's voice always found him, wherever he had wandered off to. "Come, my boy, the cows!" Or a cry like a thunderclap: "Boy, the cows are in the cornfield."

The clackety-clack of the train wheels now blended in his mind with the clang of the empty milk pails he used to help the hired man carry. He could still see and hear the warm milk gushing into the pails until they brimmed, foaming.

At the end of the day, how tired he had been. Even in the morning he had been tired, tired, tired. In the low attic bedroom where he slept, he would hear a banging on the stovepipe in the kitchen. He would open his eyes in disbelief that it was already dawn. "Four o'clock, boy!" his uncle's voice cajoled him. "Time to get up."

But he had just gone to bed, he thought, drawing on his scratchy farmer's shirt and blue jean overalls. Well, someday he would be as strong as Uncle James, or Uncle Enos, he consoled himself.

They had promised him he would, and he believed it.

[*12*]

"Adventures make strong men," they said. "Work is an adventure that makes strong men. Add 'tired' to 'tired'," they said, "and you will see."

Well, it was true. He was a man now, and he was strong. He had energy enough for ten, he thought, stretching and taking a long, deep breath. He would need both for the task ahead!

He wore a man's shoes and a store-bought suit and carried a wide-brimmed, soft man's hat and a winter overcoat. The overcoat looked a little shabby, to be sure, but that was because he had taken off the fine mink collar his mother had sewed onto last year's coat. Now the fur collar and a couple of calfbound books from his father's library rested on the shelves of Old Man Perry, the pawnbroker. The money, $7 after he had bought his railroad ticket, was in his pocket.

On the luggage rack overhead was a battered carpetbag into which he had stuffed a few clothes and his drawing tools and materials—T square, triangle, pencils, a pad of drafting paper. What else did he need? Nothing but ambition, of which he had plenty, he thought. He was on his way.

The sun sank lower in the sky. The hills and valleys began to level out. Grade crossings began to appear with more regularity. They must be approaching the Illinois line, he thought, finally leaving Wisconsin behind.

It had seemed an endlessly long winter. The snow had been piled high most of the time in great white drifts across the University of Wisconsin campus. Often he looked up from his books or his drawing board to rest his eyes on the great white world of snow outside—this world that waited, it seemed, as he was waiting for spring to come.

There was no slackening of work, of study, of talk. In the drafty engineering classrooms, problems in solid geometry were a welcome challenge to his eager mind and swift, sure pencil. In the library there was always another volume of Emerson's essays to pore over, or John Ruskin to read and reread on architecture, or Thoreau discoursing on his beloved Walden Pond. In the common room, around a coal fire with pipe smoke thickening the air, there was talk of the issues of the day, and the pros and cons of a young Wisconsin liberal named Bob LaFollette whose first term in Congress was making history for his native state. The Down East Yankees and effete New Yorkers were going to have to make room for "newcomers" west of the Mississippi. Wait and see! everyone said. Or there was talk of the coming dance or of a skating party on the frozen lake or of a church supper.

He liked it all right, but something was missing. More and more often he began to wonder what he was doing there at Madison. He wasn't really getting anywhere, he felt. No one else seemed to have his ideas. No one seemed to be able any more to teach him the things he so badly wanted to know. He yearned to be out in the world where things were happening. Where he could help things happen, not only in architecture but in—well, he didn't know exactly. All he knew was that he was beginning to feel the way he felt when he'd outgrown a jacket or a pair of pants. Everything too tight and too small. He wanted to break out somehow.

"Don't you understand, Mother," he would say, "it's not *real*. Not like the work on the farm was real. I need experience, Mother," he would say. "Real experience, if I'm ever going to be an architect."

"Patience, son," his mother would answer firmly. "You need an education, too."

He would go right on arguing, even though by this time he ought to have known it was useless. "But I'm not getting it here. It's not an education. It's plain snobbery. It's a sham. No matter what you say, I'm an outsider here. I don't belong. It's not my world, Mother, don't you understand?"

No, she didn't. So he tried to explain.

"It's not my world," he repeated. "I don't belong in classrooms. Besides, I don't want to be a minister, or a teacher, or a lawyer, or a doctor, or even an engineer. I want to be an architect. I can learn more about architecture from the study of a tree than from all these fancy generalities about culture and art. Don't you see?"

No, she didn't. Or perhaps she did, but she had her heart set on his getting an education.

"Education!" he exclaimed in exasperation. "You spell it with a capital "E" and think there's some kind of special magic in it. Well there isn't. Not for me, at any rate."

If they could have afforded to send him East, his mother dreamed on, where there were schools of architecture, then maybe. . .

"I'd simply have more to unlearn," he said. Marking time, was what he called it to himself. And he was sick of it. But for his mother's sake, he would manage somehow to last out the winter.

It had been a long cold winter, like all Wisconsin winters. He was forever turning up the mink collar around his neck. He was forever putting on and taking off galoshes, knocking the snow and ice off his heels before climbing the wooden stairs to the steamy, warm offices of Allen D. Concover, Contractor and Dean of Engineering at the University, who was kind enough to employ him after classes and on weekends as helper, odd-job man, and very junior apprentice.

The social life was pleasant enough. In spite of what he had said about being an outsider, he was as well-liked as any other soph. He dressed up in a white tie, black suit, and patent-leather pumps and took his cousin May White to the class Prom. He enjoyed the musical parties they had at home with his mother and sisters and their friends. He was a great one for amateur theatricals.

Most of all, though, the long nights of reading in his attic bedroom got him through the long winter of waiting.

The spring of 1887 had seemed slow in coming. Ice on the lakes lasted until well into February; it was the beginning of March before the great migration of birds on their way to the north country began. Spring was a time of change, of growth, of rebirth. Sleeping living things in all of nature stirred and turned over, came awake, and began to move. As Frank Lloyd Wright watched spring come once more to Wisconsin—watched and listened and felt and thought and studied and worked—impatience grew in him until he could no longer contain it. It was time for *him* to stir, to turn over, to come awake. It was time for *him* to move. Now or never!

"But Frank, you are only 18! You are too young for the city. Your Uncle says . . ." his mother's voice pursued him into his room, and he would shut the door against it, and open his books once more.

But he knew his Mother was wrong. And he knew that his Uncle, dark-bearded Uncle "Jenk," the Chicago preacher, was wrong. He was not too young. Everything was as ready to ripen in him, he felt, and to grow as was the seed of the young prairie grass swaying in the open plains the train sped by. More than that, the dream he had within him was ready to open and grow, to burst upon the waiting world with the logic of a sunrise.

The "sun of architecture" was surely rising. He quoted to himself, as he was again and again to do in the years ahead, the words of his childhood hero, Victor Hugo, the great French poet, novelist, and playwright whose prophecy he believed. The sun of architecture was surely rising and Frank Lloyd Wright intended to be there when it rose. He intended to be part and parcel of it, to be part and parcel of the great American dawn which awaited him.

"When you know what the truth is, you have to choose it," he had told himself, pacing back and forth in his attic bedroom trying to make up his mind.

"*Truth against the world!*" This was the substance of the sermon one or another of his uncles or his Welsh Grandfather Richard preached every Sunday in the family chapel in the woods. "*Truth against the world!*" was the Lloyd-Jones motto brought a generation ago from faraway Wales to the Wisconsin Valley.

"*Truth Against the World*" . . . Well, the young student had learned his lesson well. Truth for him meant that the time had come to go and do it! Go and be an architect. "Become it! Be it! Do it!" he urged himself. There was no other way. Everything in him said he was ready. The others didn't understand. Well, he would show them. He was as ready as he would ever be. The time had come.

All right, then, he had done it. He had packed up and walked out, walked out on his school, his job, his family. His mother and his sisters would soon know that he had left, he thought. He would make it up to them somehow, he determined, as soon as he had a job.

He woke up with a start and with a pang of remorse for what he had left behind him. But this twinge of guilt melted away in the quickening of excitement he felt at what he saw outside the grubby window of the day coach. People around him were beginning to stir impatiently.

So they were almost there, he thought, and could hardly believe it. Across the great, flat plain barely distinguishable from the darkening sky, against the distant horizon reddened by what he knew to be blast furnaces that could turn iron ore into liquid steel one could pour as from the lip of a cup, loomed the shapes and forms, the bulk of the unknown city.

Chicago! Eternal City of the West. He would conquer it. He was ready. He squared his shoulders and adjusted his soft-flowing tie and smoothed his rather too-long bushy hair. Neat, strong knuckled fingers folded and refolded the overcoat on his lap. He reached for his broad-brimmed hat, grasped his belongings and, struggling into his overcoat, got to his feet.

The Northwestern express pulled into the Wells Street Station at 6 P. M. It had just begun to rain. Everyone was in a hurry to get where they were going. The journey was over.

It was over, for everyone, that is, except for the country boy. For him, for Frank Lloyd Wright, architect, the journey had only begun.

Chapter 2

Wanted: One Man In 10,000

One day after another went by in the gusty, dirty city on the shores of Lake Michigan until the young job hunter had only 20 cents left. His heart was rapidly sinking as he climbed the flight of stairs to the offices of the last architect on his list, Joseph Lyman Silsbee.

He hadn't wanted to tackle Silsbee because of Uncle Jenk. Silsbee was designing Chicago's fine, new All Soul's Unitarian Church, of which Uncle Jenk was pastor. If there was a turndown here, Uncle Jenk would surely hear of it. Well, there was no help for it, he thought. It would be Silsbee or nothing. Frank swallowed hard—and kept climbing.

The walls of the outer office were covered with architect's sketches drawn with a fine true line. The strokes were as clean and sure as a stand of corn waving in a Wisconsin field. It was a good sign.

Also, he liked the tall young man with a soft beard and pompadour who came swinging through the office gate, humming an air from the *Messiah* the boy knew well. The young man bent to the roll of drawings presented him and, with a grave air, turned: "Are you a minister's son?"

The question took him by surprise. Before he had had time to think of how he cleverly might answer it, he heard himself simply answering, "Yes. How did you know?"

"Because I'm one myself," said the young man with a smile. His name was Cecil Corwin. "You have a good touch," he added. "I'll be back in a minute. Silsbee is a minister's son, too."

Soon Cecil was back with the roll of drawings and a tall, rather elegantly dressed, gentle-looking man who twirled his eyeglasses from a fine gold chain dangling from his waistcoat. This was Joseph Lyman Silsbee, architect for some of Chicago's finest clients.

"Take him on as a tracer," he said. "Eight dollars a week."

Before the year was out, the young draftsman was once again to feel the need to stir, to flex his muscles, to move on. Within a matter of months, his footsteps descending the cast-iron staircase would take him forever out of the quiet offices of the gentle-faced, aristocratic, displaced Easterner, Joseph Silsbee.

But neither Frank nor his new friend Cecil saw that far ahead on that first April morning. Nor would it have made any difference if they had. True friendship survives many blows and changes. Theirs did. An hour after their first meeting, they were seated together over a table in Kinsley's Chophouse. Corn-beef hash had never looked so good to Frank.

This was more like it! the boy thought. Already the discouragement and dismay that had kept him company during his first four days in Chicago began to fade. Eight dollars a week was less than he had hoped for, but at least it would buy him more than the doughnuts and coffee he had been eating for every meal. It would buy him a room a little better than the 75-cent-a-night one he had had in the Briggs Hotel. The smell of cheap varnish and stale bed linen was still in his nostrils. Although his pride badgered at him to say "No," he found it hard to turn down Cecil's offer to put him up in his own home—for the time being at least—until he found his way around.

Pride or no pride, he accepted and was never sorry that he had. As he unpacked his belongings in the Corwins' clean spare bedroom, he felt warmth and confidence coming back to him once more. How close he had come to losing both in the last four days! He would never forget his first impressions of the brutal, noisy, impersonal, arrogant city! He never did.

"Dear Mother . . . " he wrote. He sat for a long time with pen in hand trying to find the right words to describe what he had seen and felt. But in the end, he gave up. He simply told her he was fine and had a job. Also he sent her a $10 bill, borrowed from Cecil, to be sure, but he would pay it back, he assured his friend.

Cecil smiled at him, and the last load went off the boy's heart. He went off down the quiet South Side street to mail the letter in the corner box. He thought how different the world looked to him tonight from that first night when he had first stepped out of the Wells Street Station into the Chicago rain.

Oh, there had been an air of excitement about it, all right. Crowds brushed by him, hurrying along the wet streets as though they had somewhere to go and no time to waste getting there. The bells clanged on cable cars. He had never seen a cable car before, and of course, he had to try one right away. The street back to town was mostly mud, although here and there from the rocketing tram he glimpsed a section of wooden sidewalk and towards the center of the city paving stones had been laid. The hooves of dray horses made a great clatter and splatter across these stones, and passersby were continually dodging the sporadic rain of pebbles and mud that flew out from under the lumbering wooden wheels of vans turning a sharp corner.

The river, at night, had a certain beauty, reflecting the shimmer of lights and the orange flare of the blast furnaces. In contrast to all the hustle and bustle that took place on its banks, the river held itself aloof, it seemed to Frank. The river flowed on and was itself, no matter what. He stood in the center of the Wells Street bridge, pulled his collar up around his ears, and watched the city from a safe and isolated distance for a while like any other country boy.

He marveled at the city lights, not gas lamps like those at home, but arc lights that gave a curiously blue-white and cruel look to whatever fell within their reach. Then he climbed down off the bridge and went into a restaurant where he had a good meal because he was hungry. He walked the streets some more, looking for something he could call architecture.

He did not find any architecture, only dismal four and five story buildings with the rain washing the soot down their dingy faces. Drifting along with the unseeing crowds, he did, however, stumble upon the Chicago Opera House. In he went, as much to get out of the rain and chill and confusion as because he wanted to see the garishly advertised "Extravaganza," which turned out to be quite as gaudy and lavish as the posters announced.

Then he took a horse car ride, and then he went to his

room in the Briggs House, where he fell instantly asleep despite the smell of cheap varnish and stale bed linen and wet overshoes.

For the next three days he had got up each morning to walk the streets of the city, looking not only for a job but—hopefully still—for something he could call architecture. Not what he called gimcrack stuff, false cast-iron facades camouflaged to look like stone; cramped, box-like structures with dreary, sagging porches and beetling cornices; office buildings that looked like Renaissance cathedrals; banks that looked like Egyptian temples; mansions on fashionable Prairie Avenue that looked like 16th Century castles, or Tudor manor-houses, or French chateaux, or Queen Anne cottages.

Everything looked like something else! Where was the sun of architecture?

Chicago sweltered in midsummer heat. The lake breeze gave some relief, but was sometimes a mixed blessing, carrying as it might the sweetish-sickening odor of the stockyards.

In the rear of the old Exposition Hall where Theodore Thomas conducted concerts of light summer music—and an occasional symphony—there were round oak tables and sturdy chairs. White-coated waiters came and went with trays of beer and frankfurters, sauerkraut and boiled potatoes, great baskets of salted pretzels, kuchen and mugs of steaming coffee. It was a haven from the dust and heat that lay like a blanket over the city streets all day.

Afterwards, Frank and Cecil would walk partway home together, singing, humming—and arguing, always arguing—in the welcome darkness. Here and there a street lamp would

[23]

throw into dismal focus the object of Frank's bitter attacks. Where was the truth of architecture, he demanded, here? In this row of gingerbread houses, each on its tiny strip of cardboard lawn?

"No, Cecil, no!" he answered himself, gesticulating grandly at the offensive structures they were passing. "There's nobody home, Cecil. Nobody *lives* in these houses. Nobody at all. People just 'wear' them like a suit of clothes. Never mind if they fit or not, or if they're comfortable or not—so long as they're stylish."

"But they *are* what you call—stylish," Cecil said quietly. "They are what the best people are—"

"Wearing?" his friend interrupted with a laugh.

"All right," Cecil said. "Call it whatever you like. What's wrong with it? People want to belong, to be in the swim. They don't want to be interfered with in their ideas of what is right or fashionable or the accepted thing to do. They don't want to be upset by new ideas."

"Never mind what they want," the boy said angrily. "It's the architect's job to show them, isn't it, the difference between what is fashionable and what is right? You make fashion and rightness sound like the same thing. They're not the same thing at all, you know that. This 'accepted thing to do' —it's just another way of describing that miserable snobbery called 'Culture.' That's what causes all the trouble, 'Culture' and so-called taste. What does it amount to? I'll show you. Look—" another grand and sweeping gesture at the lean, narrow houses they were passing. "An elegant sham-show of so-called 'Queen Anne.' Gables and turrets and turnip domes and corkscrew spires and jigsaw porches. Porches that keep the light out and basements that keep the dampness in. Don't

[24]

you see it honestly for what it is, Cecil? Doesn't Silsbee see it too? If people's tastes are false and pretentious, I say— change 'em!"

Cecil laughed. "And they would say, change the architect!" he said. "Who are you going to build houses for if you give them what you think right and not what they think they want?"

"One man in 10,000 perhaps," Frank said soberly. "And some day I'll find him, the one man in 10,000 who needs me as much as I need him."

Cecil didn't answer at once. He understood his friend, but he was afraid for him. Not because he was a "radical." That part was all right. He was not the only young man in Chicago who wanted to change things, to better the world.

Chicago was a young city and growing faster than any city in the world had ever grown. In the last ten years over 500,000 newcomers had come to try their luck. The population had swelled to almost 1,000,000 by the time Frank arrived. From New England and the South, from the Far West and the Middle West, from Southern Europe, Scandinavia, and the British Isles, from anywhere and everywhere, people flocked to Chicago. Some came penniless, some came with fortunes, some came with new ideas to try out. It was a time of growth and change. The United States was becoming a nation, and Chicago was right in the middle of this new nation. Chicago was the testing ground of new techniques and new ideas: about art, culture, politics, social welfare, industry, science, and religion, about everything under the sun, it seemed.

Wherever you went, you were likely to find yourself

involved in a discussion of one sort or another. There was sure to be talk about Darwinism, for instance. Did you or did you not believe in the theory of evolution? What of industrialism and the machine age? Was capitalism to bring wealth or disaster to the common man? Fruition or frustration to the artist? What of the frontier? Were America's pioneer days over? And if so, what was to replace the missing sense of adventure?

Was the influence of the Eastern seaboard on the wane and the West coming into its own at last? In newspaper cubbyholes and furnished rooms and attics all over Chicago, young dreamers—often from the same kind of town as the boy's own Madison, Wisconsin—were struggling to put down their thoughts and hopes for the future. Prairie poets alternately sang the praises and damned the brutalities of this newest and brashest and most contradictory of cities.

Architecture, too, had its spokesmen. But they were for the most part men who had already arrived, not newcomers off the prairie, not sweating the summer out in furnished rooms, living on milk and corn-beef hash.

People only listened to an architect when he was "someone." The way people had listened to the great Bostonian, Henry Hobson Richardson. They had listened to him and imitated him, with his extravagant dress and florid manner and his unerring eye for capturing the rhythm of the Romanesque arch. They listened to the red haired Georgian, John Root and his affable engineer partner, "Uncle" Dan Burnham, pioneers in the construction of the new skyscrapers. People listened, even, to Silsbee, who brought charm and elegance and the honesty of good craftsmanship to his work. They were also beginning to listen to Louis Henri Sullivan, the only architect of any stature who had dared to break away from the traditions of the East and of the Paris school of the Beaux-Arts, where he himself had been educated.

But who would listen to the young draftsman at this stage in his career? Cecil thought. He would only be cutting his throat if he went on like this. Besides, Cecil knew, his work at the office was beginning to suffer from his discontent. "Queen Anne" or not, Silsbee was a respected man and a better architect than most.

Cecil often reminded his friend of this, but it only served to start another argument. "All the more reason," the boy would say, "for Silsbee not to lower himself to the public taste. He doesn't have to. He can do better."

This time, Cecil did not raise all the usual counter arguments. He went straight to the heart of the matter. Rather he said, "The heretic's way is not an easy one. Are you sure, at this stage, you want to choose it?"

The young rebel thought a minute seeking an honest answer. He wanted to be able to express what he really felt, not simply why he was against the houses other people built but what he himself was groping for, what his own ideas were. He was not just "against." He was also "for." He tried to put it in words.

"Cecil," he said, "if what is natural is heresy, then I have no choice. For me only what is *natural* is right, not what is pretty or sentimental or even fashionable. Only what is natural. A house is meant to be lived in, Cecil. It ought to have some meaning to the life of the people who live in it. Never mind the 'picture' it makes. A house is not made to hang on a wall or appear in the pages of fashionable magazines. A house is made to live in, isn't it?"

[27]

"No one could argue with that," Cecil admitted.

"Well, then," said the boy, "it ought to satisfy man's living needs as naturally and with as little waste motion and as much beauty as a tree satisfies its life needs, don't you see? The leaves, the branches, the twigs, the roots—they all have function to perform. It ought to be the same with a house. Nothing false, nothing for effect. Beauty yes, but . . ."

"But what, my friend?"

"I don't know how to say it, yet, Cecil. But I'm sure I'm right. Someday I'll find out—not only how to say it but how to build it. Everything must be true to its own nature, that's one thing I'm sure of, and not try to be something else."

"Or somebody else," Cecil added ruefully, thinking of his flamboyant friend. Would he ever be tamed? Cecil rather hoped not, in spite of himself.

"Least of all somebody else," Frank agreed. "One has to be oneself, doesn't one? That, at least!"

"What deep waters we two ministers' sons wander into!" Cecil laughed.

The solemn spell was broken, and the rest of the way home they sang Gilbert and Sullivan at each other at the top of their lungs until an irate householder leaned out of a second-story window and asked them how in tarnation they expected a body to get to sleep with all that infernal racket going on.

In a way Cecil was right, too, the boy admitted; he really ought to count his blessings now and then, he told himself as he let himself into his own front door. Chicago *had* been good to him. He was enjoying his life. He liked his boss even if he didn't like the houses he designed. He'd had two raises and with the last one he'd been able to send for his mother and sisters. Jennie had a job teaching school and Maginel would join them soon. They were together again in this pleasant suburban house in Oak Park—only a half-hour train ride from the Loop, but it was heaven in contrast to the hectic city.

He had friends, went to parties. He had even found a girl.

Well, then, why couldn't he be patient? If a dream was worth dreaming, it was worth waiting for, wasn't it?

Only—how long?—Frank wanted to know—would he have to wait?

Chapter 3

No One Like Sullivan

Anna Wright, sitting in her pleasant parlor in the pleasant red brick house on Forest Avenue in the pleasant tree-lined Chicago suburb of Oak Park on the edge of the prairie, sighed and told herself to stop worrying and get supper on the stove.

She drew the parlor curtains shut, lit the lamp, straightened the chintz cushions on the settee, and saw that the coal fire was properly laid in the grate. Cecil would be coming out with her son tonight, as he often did after work. With Jennie coming home soon from her teaching job and Miss Chapin, who shared the house with them, home soon from church, there'd be quite a gathering around the kitchen table. And no doubt music afterwards. Anna Wright had a lot to be thankful for, she told herself sternly.

Also—she told herself with equal austerity—it was time for her to let her son grow up. She sighed and felt a vague sense of grief and longing. The old days had gone by. There was nothing she could do about it. He was no longer a boy.

She had always said she intended her son to be an architect, even before he was born. So that he would open his newborn eyes on the inspiration of beautiful buildings, she had carefully scissored out of a magazine ten wood cuts of

English cathedrals. She had framed them and hung them on the walls of the room that was to be his nursery in the house in Richland Center, Wisconsin, where he was born June 8, 1869.

She remembered coming home from the Philadelphia Centennial in 1876 when he was seven, bringing with her the set of kindergarten blocks. They were called "Gifts," she remembered, Froebel's "Gifts," which gave her small son his first sense of what fingers and imagination could do with cubes, triangles, and squares. And all the colors of the rainbow besides!

She had sent him to her father and brothers' farm in the Valley, so that he could learn the lessons of nature and grow to be a man, free from cant and hypocrisy, feeling at home in the woods and the fields, with other growing things. Finally, she had sold her home in Madison and come to be here at his side, to make a new home for him here, for the family. For Jennie, and for Maginel who would soon follow. It was quite like old times, she thought. But it wasn't really. Things had changed.

She had known her son would be an architect even before he was born. And now he was one. He had a right to grow up. Just the same, it was hard sometimes. He was so impetuous—well, not impetuous exactly, but so sure of himself, of what he wanted.

Now, for instance, he would soon be wanting a home of his own. All signs pointed in that direction. Catherine Tobin—Kitty, as he called her—was a nice girl, pretty and vivacious, well brought up. And she loved him.

But marriage was a responsibility. No one knew this better than Anna Wright. Her son knew it too. For the last five years he had had to be the man of the family, ever since his father had turned on his heel one day and left the house, never to return.

No, she thought, that was not an altogether fair way to put it, even to herself. William Wright had left the house five years ago because she had asked him to. "Well, Mr. Wright," she had said, "leave us. Go your way. We will do the best we can."

How long ago it seemed! Anna sighed. In those days people didn't talk about love as freely as they did now, Anna reflected ruefully. One admired a man, respected him, felt proud to be at his side. All these things she had felt for her husband.

William Cary Wright, Frank's father, was an educated man, an Easterner, born and bred in his father's Connecticut ministry. At Amherst College he had studied to prepare for medicine, then for the law. But his poetic nature needed other fields to flower in, and when Anna met him he was a wandering music master, earning a bare living in the frontier towns of the Middle West. Pupils were few and far between, and William confided to his wife that sometimes he felt a longing to return to his father's calling, and to the East. So they went, William, Anna, Frank, Jennie.

But William Wright was not cut out to be a preacher either, and back they all trooped to Wisconsin. This time to a shingled cottage by the edge of Lake Mendota in Madison, a growing university town. A musical academy ought to attract pupils here.

Anna Wright was hopeful once more. But it was no use. William had always been a strange and lonely man. He grew more so with the years. And he was a perfectionist! "No,

Frank!" she would hear him saying to their son. "Get it *right!* not half right, *all* right. Again now."

His son's fingers, already better skilled to hold a pencil or to build cathedrals and clean, long-lined block houses with the Froebel "Gifts," would once again begin to march across the piano keys, would finally begin to discover the structure of the music that he played.

Alone in his room, with the music he preferred above all things—and seemingly above most people—William Wright began to closet himself more and more from the world. Of course his pupils dropped away sooner or later. Anna sighed. She didn't blame William for his failure to make a go of things. Deep down, she wondered if somehow she had failed him. It was no use trying to understand him. It was no use going on. And still, in spite of it all, when she had finally said, "Well, leave us then, Mr. Wright!" she had not really believed that he would do so. But he had.

Her son too had dark moods. Frank too dreamed of perfection and was impatient with anything which fell short of it. He, too, was unwilling to compromise.

But the boy loved life, she told herself. He never turned away from experience. He grasped everything that came his way. He—

As if in answer to her unspoken thoughts, the front door burst open and her son came like a whirlwind into the kitchen, lifted her up, and whirled her about in the air.

"Mother!" he cried. "I'm going to work for Louis Sullivan. The 'Master'—he's taken me on!"

There was no lack of laughter or of music in the Wright house at Oak Park that night. Only Cecil seemed to hold him-

[*33*]

self a little apart from the gaiety.

"We'll still be friends," Frank threw an arm around his shoulder. "You'll see, we'll be better friends than ever. How much we'll have to talk about now. There's no one like Sullivan. Oh, and how he dressed and . . . "

Whereupon he put on a fine show for them of how the Master looked, with his little pointed beard and his great, dark eyes and his fine brown suit, how he strutted not to appear as short as he was, and how haughtily he spoke to his draftsmen, as though they were nobodies. Frank even showed how the draftsmen, bent over their drawing boards, turned their heads just a fraction of an inch to get a look at this brash newcomer who was going to beat them all cold, the most talented, the greatest, the up-and-coming genius, Frank Lloyd Wright.

Even Cecil joined in the laughter and applause that followed. Silsbee would be hurt, Cecil knew, and with reason. Silsbee had been a good boss to the boy and a good friend. Well, it couldn't be helped.

Cecil, loyal to the core, was proud of his friend's achievement but troubled. Others besides Silsbee would be hurt, he feared, as Frank Lloyd Wright trod his path to greatness. Well, it couldn't be helped, he told himself once more. He knew how his friend had longed to work for Sullivan, how much he admired him. Could he be blamed if he took advantage of the opening when it came? Wouldn't anyone else have done the same?

Besides, the boy was right. There was no one else like Sullivan—unconventional, poetic, arrogant, a genius some said. No one else like Sullivan, Cecil thought, except—perhaps—Frank himself.

[34]

Chapter 4

"Form Follows Function!"

Haughty, egotistical, cold as he might seem to the outsider, Louis Henri Sullivan burned with ideas and enthusiasms. He loved and hated with equal passion. Part Irish and part French, he liked to talk. He embroidered his speech with something very close to poetry at times. At other times his ideas came out as straight and clean as the blow of a hammer.

"Form follows function!" he would say, informing a hapless client that he was not interested in learning of anyone's preference for Colonial, Renaissance, Gothic, Greek, Tudor, Louis XIVth, or Egyptian.

By this he meant that, first of all, a building was supposed to do the job it was wanted for. That was its function. That came first. The so-called "form" ought to follow naturally. It ought not to be arbitrarily imposed on the building like a costume to be worn to a fancy dress ball. This was a revolutionary idea in architecture in the 1890's. People didn't really understand it, although they quoted it with admiration or derision everywhere. People thought the outside of a building was what came first. Then the architect worried about the inside later. Sullivan didn't agree.

When Frank Lloyd Wright came into the firm of Adler & Sullivan as a draftsman at $25 a week, designs for the great Auditorium Building were well under way. The Auditorium, with its vast concert hall seating 4,000 people, went a long way towards proving Sullivan's point for those who had eyes to see it. Although Sullivan did not know it at the time, the Auditorium was to be the high point of his career.

On that gala night of December 9th, 1889, even the President of the United States, Benjamin Harrison, and his First Lady joined Chicagos' leading citizens in celebrating the Auditorium's opening. Adelina Patti, America's favorite soprano, stepped up to the footlights to sing "Home Sweet Home," and a hush fell over the audience. Tears glistened and diamonds glittered. Then came the ovation. For Frank Lloyd Wright, 20 years old, and already the "pencil in his master's hand," it was a never-to-be-forgotten experience.

The Auditorium deserved the fame it got. Sullivan's partner, Dankmar Adler, was a brilliant engineer, as down to earth and practical as Sullivan was imaginative and mercurial. For the Auditorium, Adler designed an acoustical "shell" that carried the fullness and the purity of sound without distortion to every corner of the great hall. Sullivan, true to his "Form follows function" credo, disciplined the lines and masses of his structure to fall within a clean and simple design. There were no turrets or fancy gables or cornices or cupolas. Its very cleanness suggested power and strength. But, because Sullivan was, after all, artist as well as builder, the severity of the building blossomed into a web of lyric beauty with the addition of the ornament Sullivan knew how to draw so well.

Above the Auditorium, a tower building soared 19-stories high, above the lake and the sprawling city. At the very top were the new Adler and Sullivan offices. Here for almost seven years, Wright worked at the side of his beloved Master. *"Lieber Meister,"* Dear Master, he called him, a term of affection as well as respect. Here, for almost seven years, Wright worked and learned—and listened.

Long after the day's work was over, the two men would sit in the darkening offices, looking out over the wind-tumbled waters of Lake Michigan or the jewel-like lights of the city. Sullivan never seemed to run out of things to say. At times Frank thought to himself that the Master talked more to express his own feelings and thoughts than to communicate them to his young disciple.

It didn't matter, though. This was a side of Sullivan very few people knew. The boy had sensed it from the very beginning, from the first day he had walked into the office. Sullivan had not only studied his drawings with interest but had shown him his own. What an honor! And what a genius Sullivan was! All his passion and all the lyrical, sensitive qualities he concealed behind his haughty exterior flowered in the immensely complicated and yet free-flowing drawings. Details of arches, of ornaments as well as the whole line, the whole concept of a building came magically to life under Sullivan's pencil.

The young architect wasn't so free in the beginning. The geometry of the triangle, the cube, and the sphere was as much, if not more, a part of him then as it had been in the days of the Froebel "Gifts." Sullivan saw that this was a good thing, but he also saw the youth had not yet learned to let his talent come out freely and easily, naturally.

"Make it come alive, man!" Sullivan clapped him on the back as he sat at his drawing board. "Make it come alive!"

He learned to make his drawings sing as the Master's

[37]

did, and in the end it was hard sometimes to tell one's work from the other's. If one looked closely, though, he saw that underneath the delicately wrought designs the youth worked from Sullivan's sketches, there was still a fundamental geometry, a kind of basic simplicity that was his alone. Each man had his own style, of course; the young draftsman was gradually discovering his.

"No two men are alike," Sullivan said. "In plain words —each human being is unique."

This uniqueness of the human being was something Sullivan thought American democracy ought to care deeply about and protect. It was not always happening that way at the turn of the century. The great move was on towards lumping people together in organizations: in labor unions, in huge corporations, in enormous factories, in cities. Something was being lost, left out, Sullivan thought, as the machine began to take over. "Our civilization," he said, "should rest squarely on man's quality of virtue as a *human being*."

Others thought so too, even though at the time it seemed a losing battle. Ideals were changing as America itself was changing from a rural to an industrial nation; and progress, then as now, always seems to bring with it a certain amount of confusion in men's minds.

Although Frank Lloyd Wright did not share Sullivan's fear of the machine age, he did agree that it was more important than ever for a man not to lose sight of his own individuality, not to get lost in the crowd. He remembered the crowds of unseeing, faceless faces that had greeted him on his arrival in Chicago that rainy night long ago. He did not want to be one of them. He couldn't have been even if he had wanted to. He wasn't made that way.

To the motto of his Lloyd-Jones uncles and aunts—
"Truth against the world"—he now added one that seemed to
suit him better: "Truth is Life." He had had this motto carved
on the great oak slab above the fireplace of the new house he
had built for himself and Kitty Tobin—Mrs. Frank Lloyd
Wright—on Forest Avenue in the old Oak Park woodlot.

No sooner was the carving finished than he wondered
to himself if he hadn't meant "Life is Truth," but it was too
late to change it. It was a hard motto to live up to either way,
he thought, and remembered something that had happened
to him as a child. At the time he had puzzled over it a lot. Now
it began to make sense.

Walking hand-in-hand with one of his uncles over a
snowy hillside, he had broken away suddenly because he
caught sight of a patch of milkweed and of tasseled grasses
sticking their heads up out of the white expanse. Off he wandered, this way and that, gathering the pods and the tassels
and the long golden stalks until his arms were full. Then he
ran proudly back to his uncle with his treasure.

But the uncle was displeased and, turning the boy by the
arm, made him look backwards. There he saw two very
different sets of footprints in the snow. His uncle's firm
footprints made a straight, unwavering line to where they
both now stood. His own footprints searched and rambled,
crossing and recrossing his uncle's like a vine on a tree trunk,
he thought. The uncle was proud of the straight, purposeful
path his feet had made. He meant it to be a lesson to Frank,
and it was. But it was not the kind of lesson his uncle
had meant it to be.

No two men can take the same path, Frank now thought.
Each must find his own way. The small boy's way gave him

[39]

an armful of treasures at the end. It was the explorer's way. It was still the youth's way. Perhaps it always would be. It was also the poet's way, free and singing as he went.

It was hard to say whether he learned more at the drawing board or from his endless conversations with the Master. Sometimes they would leave the office together after dark, still talking, and ride together along Lake Shore Drive where the millionaires' mansions were beginning to go up, one by one. In the open carriage under a night sky, they would quote poetry to each other. Sullivan had introduced him to the world of Walt Whitman. "Leaves of Grass" and the "Song of Myself" said precisely the things Sullivan was feeling, and the things the youth knew that he himself wanted to express in the buildings he would create.

A man ought to be free and unfettered by false conventions. Why wear a celluloid collar and a stiff tie when a soft shirt and a flowing tie sat more easily? A man ought not to be bound by false ideals that robbed him of his dignity. Why worship things that other people worshipped just because it was fashionable to do so? In the great new nation of America, "No man a master, no man a slave", was what Whitman said. Frank Lloyd Wright and Sullivan agreed.

In the world of architecture, this was easier said than done. People were still slaves, although they might not know it, chained to a tradition that no longer had meaning for them. Imitators still imitated other imitators. As Wright had said to Cecil in his first Chicago days—everything looked like something else.

"What are people afraid of?" Frank wondered. "Of being themselves?" "Yes, that's it, all right!" Sullivan, in his

own way, said the same thing. It was the end of an e
van said, and the beginning of a new one. What kind
one? Well, Sullivan's hopes were high. At least, in architecture, he hoped he might show the way out of imitation of the
past into something honestly of today. Why should a skyscraper look like a cathedral? It ought to look like a skyscraper, he said, and he built one that *did* look that way.
It was the Wainwright Building in St. Louis. Tall and
slender, it did not try to disguise its tallness, did not rely on
horizontal masses of stone to disguise the verticality of the
steel skeleton within. "The essence of a tall building is its
tallness," Sullivan said.

Wright listened, watched, and learned that an honest
building, like an honest person, has to grow from inside.
Nothing could be added to make it right if the idea was
wrong. The idea of the Wainwright Building was its tallness.
The logic of a skyscraper was that it enabled light and air to
reach into the lives of the people who worked there, high
above the soot and commotion of the city streets.

What then was the kind of logic to apply to the homes
people lived in, he wondered. Soon he would have a chance
to find out for himself, to try his own wings. The office of
Adler and Sullivan was not primarily interested in building
houses. Commercial buildings were their specialty. The youth
had the field to himself—and the confidence of his Master
that he could handle it.

"Form follows function" was Sullivan's way. It became
Wright's way, too. It made sense.

The Charnley House went up before Wright was 25.
Officially it bore the signature of the firm of Adler and Sulli-

van, but unofficially and unmistakably it bore the stamp of its designer, Frank Lloyd Wright. Astor Street, where it stood, boasted a row of new residential mansions, each one more Victorian than the next. There were the usual bay windows and gables, elaborate cornices and dormer windows.

Not so the Charnley house. It was almost austere in its simplicity. The long unbroken line of its facade, the soft tones of its buff-colored Roman brick and seasoned limestone, the slender balcony and strong, clean roof lines, all combined to give it an air of serenity. It was a restful house and managed to make the neighboring houses look overdressed and fussy. It had a new kind of spacious elegance about it. Nothing looked cramped, nothing forced, nothing false.

It was not a perfect house by any means, not perfect, that is, in the sense Frank Lloyd Wright wanted it to be. There was something lacking, something he would later discover, he knew. For all its startling appearance of being fresh and modern and understated—geometrical almost— it didn't altogether satisfy the young architect.

There was still something he had to learn, something he had left out. What was it? The proportions were good, he knew. Gone was the long, tall, cramped look most Chicago houses had. No matter how vast some of these houses might be, to Wright they always seemed to be perched on top of the ground, as though they had no connection with the earth, but were just sort of stuck up there like decorations. The Charnley house didn't look perched. It looked comfortable and settled, not as if the first high wind would blow it away.

Still—Wright wasn't satisfied. He would have to find

out why. He went back to his drawing board.

Evening after evening, with the fire blazing in the hearth of the Oak Park house, while Kitty played Bach or Beethoven on the new Steinway grand, Wright went back to the drawing board. Other houses followed, done mostly in his spare time because the firm kept him busy with other work.

The houses were good. People liked them. They helped to pay the bills. But still Wright wasn't satisfied. And it wasn't very long before he went back, not only to the drawing board, but to Nature.

Chapter 5

A Parting of the Ways

Kano was a young black stallion with a will of his own. Frank Lloyd Wright, his new master, also had a will of his own, and so the two inevitably had their ups and downs. Nevertheless, they soon became the best of friends. He liked nothing better in the long late autumn afternoons than to saddle up Kano and ride out across the plains toward the setting sun.

By this time, the Forest Avenue cottage in Oak Park overflowed with children. It was also beginning to overflow with bills. Frank Lloyd Wright was "Papa" to six young Lloyd Wrights: Lloyd, John, Catherine, David, Frances, and Llewellyn. And "Papa's" children had to have the best.

No one ever seemed to dispute this point, least of all the butcher, the grocer, the baker, the music teachers, the department store clerks, the tailor, the dressmaker, the bookseller, the art dealer, and a host of others who happily saw to it that life in the house on Forest Avenue was filled with the best of all possible things for a growing family—and for a father who knew what the best was when he saw it.

An enormous willow tree grew right up through the roof of the corridor connecting the house with the newly built Studio. Neighbors began to call the Wright place "The House with the Tree."

The Studio too was soon overflowing—with work, happily, and with some things Frank Lloyd Wright liked to have near him when he worked: a bronze statuette, a Chinese bowl holding a sheaf of autumn leaves or wild flowers from the prairie, a window ledge lined with books, a folio of prints and drawings.

Now and then the studio also overflowed with clients conferring around the big central table. Even more often the studio overflowed with children, escapees from what he called "Catherine's kindergarten establishment" next door. "Papa's" children loved to climb up onto the balcony that went around the great two-storied drafting room and peer down hopefully to see what was going on.

Life for Frank Lloyd Wright was exuberant and full. It was also strenuous, and sometimes exasperating. He was never alone except in the small hours of the night or in the late afternoon when he would lay down his pencil, bid a client good-day, wipe a small child's nose, shove a copy of Whitman's poems in his pocket, saddle Kano, and be off.

Eventually, Kano learned to respect his master's moods. He learned not to stop all of a sudden when Frank Lloyd Wright wanted to keep on going. He learned not to keep on going when Frank Lloyd Wright wanted to stop, to pull the book out of his pocket, and to read. Together master and stallion would linger on the prairie until darkness fell; the master, no longer able to read the words he loved so well, would pocket the book, go on quoting to himself from memory as long as he could, lay the reins gently on Kano's neck, and head for home. Now Kano could run to his heart's content, and generally he did!

Kano bore his name as proudly as had his faraway-and-long-ago namesake—the first of a long line of Japanese land-scape painters. Frank called the stallion Kano because, as the art of Japan began to be discovered by the Western world, he was spellbound by this discovery. Across centuries, seas, and continents, the art of Japan seemed to reach out directly to him, and to add its voice to those he had already heard— the music of Beethoven, the words of Victor Hugo, the songs of Whitman, the design of Louis Sullivan, the architecture of a tree.

Frank was never sure exactly how or when he had come to discover the art of Japan. It did not really matter very much. The point was that it had happened and that it became a part of him forever.

The great Columbian Exposition of 1893 had come and gone. Called the "White City," this vast array of exhibition halls had been modelled after the architectural period generally known as "Classical." The main buildings surrounding the Great Court simulated Greek and Roman temples. A coat of white paint laid lavishly over the stucco facades gave the "City" its nickname. Everything in sight was decorated with gold trim. Just for good measure, the Administration Building had a giant dome. Crowds came from everywhere. The Fair was a colossal success. It won prestige and it made money. But for those interested in the future of honest architecture in America, the Fair was a disaster.

"Thus architecture died in the land of the free and the home of the brave!" declared Louis Sullivan and predicted that it would take half a century for the damage to be repaired. He was nearly right.

For nearly half a century, public buildings followed the fashion set by the "White City." Graeco-Roman banks and domed state capitols and porticoed and be-columned Chambers of Commerce, libraries and post office buildings sprang up all over the country. "Form follows function" fell by the wayside. Sullivan, almost overnight, became a broken man.

But Frank Lloyd Wright was only beginning, and the Fair held discovery for him, and inspiration. He did not find either of these things, of course, in the buildings of the Great Court, nor even particularly in Louis Sullivan's Transportation Building, on which he himself had worked and with which he was therefore thoroughly familiar. No, it was something quite different.

The Ho-o-den Pavilion, a wooden temple, official exhibit of the Imperial Japanese Government, stood by itself on the Wooded Island in the midst of an artificial lake. Crossing the gently arched bridge onto this island was like stepping into another world. Strangely enough, this world did not seem foreign to Frank Lloyd Wright. On the contrary, it seemed to confirm many of the deepest feelings he had always had about the relationship of art and architecture to life and to nature. He felt utterly at home on the Island. Here within the framework of an ancient culture was the simplicity of line he understood so well. Here also was evidence that the soul, the mind, the eye of man understood and revered the beauty of the natural world. The placing of a flower in a vase, a spray of plum blossoms in early spring sun, the starkness of the pines on a snowy mountain, all these had meaning in the art of Japan. Nothing in Japanese art or architecture denied nature. Everything admitted it.

"If it's not *natural*, it's not right!" Frank Lloyd Wright could hear himself saying to Cecil, gesturing dramatically in

[47]

the middle of the dimly lit suburban street on a long past summer evening. And he could hear Cecil's equally dramatic and solemn answer that heresy, particularly in matters of taste, was a dangerous thing.

Was it heresy then to have an idea in one's head about a house being "natural"? Frank Lloyd Wright did not think it was, and he wanted badly to prove that he was right. What did he mean by a natural house? Cecil had wanted to know. Wright had not been able to answer him then. Was he any closer to the answer now? He thought he was.

Nature was just another word, after all, and people used it to mean an infinite number of things. The question was what did *he* mean by it, not only in an abstract sense because he was not simply trying to define a word or describe an idea. He was trying to describe a house, and a house—when you came right down to it—was not only an idea in one's head. It was a fact, and a very tangible one.

Well, then what *did* he mean by a natural house? First of all, he knew what he did *not* mean by it. He did not mean that an architect ought to imitate Nature. He did not mean that an architect ought to build a tree or a human body or imitate either. But he did mean that a house ought to do the job it was meant to do as a tree or a human body did the jobs they were meant to do. So he began to think about a house as though he had never seen one. He tried to define it. What was a house? And what was the job it was meant to do?

A house was simply a machine to live in, he decided. Just as a human body was a machine, as a tree was a machine. If a house was going to "work" as smoothly and efficiently as a human body or as a tree, each of its parts ought to be as intimately conneccted as part were in Nature. Every detail of a house ought to be organically a part of the whole design, as an arm or a leg were part of the human body, as a branch and its leaves were part of the tree. A house ought to give a smooth and flowing feeling, any easy feeling. It ought to look as though it had always been where it was. It ought to look and to feel right, natural. (There was that word "natural" again! He never got very far from that word all his life.)

He began to think then of what actually made a house seem natural, as though it had always been where it was. First of all, it ought to have some relationship to the natural conditions that surrounded it. A house did not exist in a vacuum. It existed somewhere, and the "somewhere" was the first important thing to think about.

Commuting back and forth on the suburban line between Chicago and Oak Park, or riding across the prairie on Kano's back, Wright could not fail to notice that most houses stuck up out of the landscape like sore thumbs. Tall, lean buildings had no relationship with the vast plains or gently rolling prairies. Skinny, rickety looking chimneys stuck up into the enormous sky. Not only were they offensive to the eye. They were also meaningless, because the houses contained no real fireplaces.

The prairie winters were cold, windy, bleak. Skies were gray from November to March. What could be nicer than coming home to a great roaring fire in the fireplace? Instead of this, most people came home to a mantelpiece and a fake hearth. Sometimes the opening cut into the wall under the fake mantelpiece was laid with fake logs from which a blue gas flame fluttered wanly. Yes, many houses had steam heat by now, and electricity too, but there was something about the *feeling* of a great log fire burning deep in the heart

[49]

of the house. There was something comforting about it. A fire in the fireplace meant home, permanence, love, and security, and the cosy feeling that came with belonging.

But a house ought to be more than shelter from sun and rain, heat and cold. It ought not only to separate people from the extremes of Nature. It ought also to bring people and Nature back together again in the kind of intimacy and with the kind of respect that was so dear to the Japanese.

It was not necessary for man to declare himself Nature's enemy and to barricade himself against her. On the contrary, there was comfort and a sense of belonging too to be derived from closeness to Nature. Frank Lloyd Wright had always known that.

Yes, man was unique. He was neither a plant, nor an animal, nor a stone, nor a brook. Yet he was part of all these things, too. He belonged to the land as surely as the land belonged to him. Why should his house separate him from it?

Why should his house be made of materials twisted and tortured into looking like something they were not? Wood should look like wood, stone like stone, brick like brick. Now there were new materials to build with, and new machines to work with. Machines ought to be used to bring out the true beauty of a material, not to falsify and disguise it.

Finally, he began to think more and more about the inside of a house. The inside was where people lived, wasn't it? The inside was where the house began to do its work. If the inside weren't right, weren't natural, then nothing would be really right or natural about the house.

He thought about the insides of the houses people were building every day and then condemned to live in for a lifetime. Between the usual four box-like outer walls was an inner series of box-like rooms. Some had oblong holes punched in the walls for windows. Some had larger holes for doors. The insides of the houses people lived in were like a series of little cardboard boxes, he thought. One room had no relationship to another. They were like the little rectangular cells of a prison, he thought, and he looked for a way to help people break out of their little box-like cells.

"What the people are within, the buildings are without . . ." Sullivan had said. Frank Lloyd Wright thought that the reverse of this statement might be even truer. In other words, the insides of people's houses conformed to a false idea of what people were really like and forced them to live in a false and uncomfortable way. How could people live freely, honestly, and comfortably in a series of little cardboard boxes, closed in, with scarcely a view of the sky or the sight of green grass or a tree to lift up their hearts?

He decided to do something about it. It was time, he thought, to take another step in his long journey towards becoming an architect. He was ready to move on again. Characteristically, his moving onward was to bring with it a certain pang, a certain loss. He had not meant to come to a parting of the ways with Sullivan. He regretted it bitterly when it happened and wanted to patch things up with his Lieber Meister.

But the damage had been done. There had been a misunderstanding and Wright had lost his temper and walked out. There was no help for it once it happened. Lieber Meister refused to see him. For 12 long years they were not to meet.

From that day on, though he did not know it then, he would always go it alone. His apprenticeship was over.

Chapter 6

I'd Rather Be Free

The right to be oneself, to express oneself, Frank Lloyd Wright soon discovered, was not easily won. Nor was it won without sacrifice.

It was simple enough to rent offices and hang out a shingle proclaiming one's profession to the world at large. On the clear glass entrance door, high in the tower of a downtown Chicago building, it was simple enough to instruct a sign painter how to letter the names and tell him where to place them. In small goldleaf letters, the sign, slightly off center, read:

FRANK LLOYD WRIGHT, ARCHITECT
CECIL CORWIN, ARCHITECT

Friends, but not partners, the two young men again slipped easily back into the habits of the old days at Silsbee's. Waiting for the first clients to appear, they sat and talked each day at the great square conference table in the common room they shared. Each day an armful of fresh flowers from Wright's small Oak Park garden appeared in a large glass bowl, the room's only decoration. Each day they talked of the past, of the present, of the future. As they looked through the clear-paneled entrance door, they wondered who would be the first to take his courage into his hands and enter.

Wright's first client had courage. Also, he had faith in himself as well as in this new young architect. The client needed both, because the Winslow House burst upon suburban River Forest like an exotic flower. No one had ever seen the likes of it before. Some said Mr. Winslow had to take the back way to the station every morning to avoid the ridicule of his neighbors. Never mind. Mr. Winslow liked his house. He didn't miss the absence of fancy trimmings. He liked the long, low line, the harmonious way the brick and softly colored, delicately ornamented tiles blended with the shadows cast by the great trees across the lawns. He liked the feeling of shelter the deep eaves of the roof gave. He was not the only one who liked his house.

Across the street, surrounded by a spacious park, lived Mr. Waller. Mr. Waller, whether he knew it or not, was to play a most important part in the conflict that was soon to gather in and around Frank Lloyd Wright. Mr. Waller's great friend was "Uncle" Dan Burnham, dean of Chicago architects, chief planner of the White City and director of the Columbian Exposition.

Mr. Waller looked across the street at Mr. Winslow's house and liked what he saw. The more he looked at it, the more he liked it. His friend, Uncle Dan, agreed with him. It was a "gentleman's house," he said. Mr. Waller not only liked the house, but he liked young Wright and thought he would go far. He knew about the growing family on Forest Avenue, the six young mouths to feed and six young minds to educate. Mr. Waller had vision and he had money. He decided to invest in the young architect's future.

[53]

It was a good dinner. The company and the conversation were lively. Mr. and Mrs. Waller were the best of hosts, and the Wrights were honored to meet the Burnhams. All went swimmingly until the moment when Mr. Waller led the way into his cozy library, Uncle Dan and Wright following. Mr. Waller turned the key in the lock, for a reason which Frank Lloyd Wright never fully understood. Unless, he thought, it was to make sure that the ladies realized that this was to be a conversation in which they had no part. He was grateful, as it turned out, for the secrecy of what went on in that pleasant room. It was a long, long time before he himself had the courage to tell Kitty what had happened behind the locked library door that night.

He had no preparation for the decision he was to be asked to make. The choice was simply offered to him complete, with no ifs, ands, or buts attached to it. The gift was his. He had only to reach out and take it then and there— if he wanted it.

But did he want it? He listened. Uncle Dan, expansive, friendly, talked on:

"Four years' study at the Beaux-Arts, Frank, to begin with. Four years in Paris. Then Rome—two years in Rome. All expenses paid." The Oak Park family would be taken care of in the meantime, educated, clothed, fed; and when he got back a job would be waiting for him in Uncle Dan's office.

"Well, Frank?" Mr. Waller stopped pacing up and down the length of the study floor and looked at him with a smile.

He sat in tongue-tied silence. A dream come true! Mr. Waller had faith in him. So did Uncle Dan. They were

[54]

prepared to offer him more than confidence. The generosity of the offer took his breath away.

Yes, it was a dream come true. Only—was it *his* dream? It would bring him success, but was it the kind of success *he* dreamed of, as he sat in the Studio bending over his drawing board late into the night? Or as he paced up and down holding forth to Cecil in the tower conference room with the great square table? Or as he rode forth across the prairie at sunset? Was it?

He couldn't find the right words. He knew Uncle Dan was right, that the future of architecture would go the way of the White City, and that "success" in the ordinary sense of the word would lie in following that path—the path of Classical architecture of the Beaux-Arts, of Rome, of the great Graeco-Roman tradition.

His heart sank. If only he could talk it over with the Master. If only Sullivan were there. But he wasn't. Wright had closed that door on himself. Or had he? Could it ever really be closed? No matter what harsh words had passed between Lieber Meister and himself, Wright suddenly knew that the door Sullivan had opened for him would never now be closed. It was too late, far too late.

As if in echo to his thoughts, Uncle Dan said, "The time is now, Frank! Another year, and it will be too late!"

"It's already too late, Uncle Dan," he replied. "It's too late for me to choose success at the sacrifice of what I believe in. It would mean giving up what I believe to be the right way, don't you see? I can't—just run away," he said miserably.

"Run away from what?" Uncle Dan objected. "All the great men today believe the right way to be the Classical way. How can you hope to succeed without a knowledge of what that means? You *are* running away, my boy, if you turn your back on the education that can bring you success."

"What you choose now," Mr. Waller said, "will be with you for a lifetime, Frank. You are choosing for the rest of your life, you know."

"Yes, I do know, Mr. Waller," Wright said soberly. "That's just it. You see, I guess I just have to say that I'd rather be free—free to be myself, that is—and take my chance on failure than to go on for the rest of my life tied to the kind of success that really has nothing to do with me—or my country."

Silence fell in the room. What more was there to say? If only he could make them see it, understand that he was not just being stubborn and egotistical and ungrateful. He was grateful, but he felt as though he'd been offered a jail sentence. The locked room itself began to seem like a prison to him. He made one last effort.

"No," he said. "I didn't mean to say 'my' country. I meant to say 'our' country—America. America has to create an architecture that has meaning for us. A new, young, bold architecture that expresses the way Americans feel—not the way the Greeks or the Romans felt, or the way the French or the English feel, but the way we feel! American architecture has to belong to us and to our traditions, young as they are. That's what I'm after, don't you see?"

The silence only deepened.

"I've got to go on as I've started," Wright said. "Thank you both, but I've got to keep faith with my convictions, foolish as that may sound."

Mr. Waller unlocked the library door, opened it, and

stood aside to let him pass. Would people ever understand?

Cecil would understand, Wright thought. Here was one person he could count on. They had come a long way together. Lately, though, there had seemed less time for confidences. Work had begun to consume Wright. Sometimes it seemed to him that he ate, drank, slept, and dreamed work.

Cecil did understand. He understood Frank Lloyd Wright better than he understood himself at times. Cecil was also beginning to understand Cecil. He had come to a decision of his own. It was a painful moment for both of them.

"What is it, Cecil?" Frank said. "Do you think I was wrong?"

Cecil had a half-sad, half-funny smile on his face. "You have to be yourself, Frank. We both know that," he said quietly.

"Well then, what's the trouble?"

"I have to be myself, too, Frank. I've found there's no joy in architecture for me, not any more. Not the way there is for you—you live in your work. You are your work. I'm not. I'm—an outsider, and I guess I just want—out!"

Had he left Cecil behind? Frank asked himself. Neglected him, forgotten him, taken him too much for granted? What had happened?

"You're a good architect, Cecil. You're talking nonsense! Stay and be my partner. I need you to help me. Stay!"

"No," said Cecil. "I'll always be your friend—you know that—but I'm not the right partner for you—if there is a right one. You'll go far, Frank, but—I'm afraid for what is coming to you. I'll always be your friend when you need me.

But. . ." His voice fell away into silence.

"Stay," his friend pleaded. "I need you now."

The place would be nothing at all without Cecil. In the chill that seemed to descend upon them, Cecil said the one thing that struck deepest of all into Frank Lloyd Wright. To this he could make no reply, because there was none to make.

"You see, Frank, I can't go on watching you do the things I can't do. The heart has gone out of me. I don't want to be an architect any more. Perhaps I never did, but I didn't know that until we came in here together. Now I know it. I'm getting out. I'm going East, Frank. I believe you'll have the kind of success you want. I'll always be your friend."

Cecil went without bitterness. For no reason anyone could put a finger on, the two friends never saw each other again.

Chapter 7

"Build It"

The tower offices were nothing withoug Cecil. Wright did his best to bury the grief he felt at the loss of his friend, and so he moved in with a group of young architects in a large loft in Steinway Hall. As usual, where Frank Lloyd Wright went, excitement and controversy followed. New ideas, the formulation of new approaches to American architecture, new attitudes towards everything from the size of a chimney to the uses of a power saw came thick and fast. The talk in Steinway Hall soon overflowed to women's clubs, architectural forums, and cultural centers in and around Chicago.

In no time at all, Frank Lloyd Wright had once again asserted himself, this time going against the grain of a group of artists, artisans, and architects who saw eye-to-eye with Wright—or thought they did—on the evils of the coming machine age.

No one was more shocked or surprised at or profoundly disappointed in the lecture Frank Lloyd Wright gave to the newly formed Arts and Crafts Society at Chicago's famous Hull House, than the members of the Society themselves. They had looked for an ally if not actually a leader in Wright. Wright the great individualist would speak out for them against this new monster, technology.

But no! "The Art and Craft of the Machine" was the

first expression on the part of an American artist that the 20th century machine was not Frankenstein's monster, but simply a tool in the hands of an arist. The machine was not at fault, Wright said. People were.

"I come to you as an architect to say my word for the *right* use of machines. Grasp and use their power in a *creative sense* and their terrible forces are not antagonistic to any fine individualistic quality in man."

In spite of a stirring editorial in the Chicago *Tribune* next day applauding Wright's forthright speech, he himself was soon dropped from the ranks of the Society. It was not the first time, nor was it to be the last, that Wright found the least support for his "radical" ideas from the sources he had hoped would give him the most: the profession itself.

All right, if he had to go it alone, he would! Why go backwards when I can go forward? he argued. Why revive outworn traditions when I can create new ones? Accept change, don't fight it, master it! Why do it the way it's always been done before? If there's a better way, find it, believe in it, do it!

"Yes, *but*—" someone always said. "Will it work?"

Back home, in the Valley, an anxious family conclave of five brothers and two sisters gathered around an architect's sketches of a windmill. The windmill was to pump water for the Hillside Home School, started, owned, managed, run and taught by the two sisters, Nell and Jane Lloyd-Jones. The brothers, James, Jenkin, Enos, John, and Philip, stood around and argued. The sketch of the windmill, a tower in the trees on a hilltop, bore no resemblance whatsoever to any windmill anyone had ever seen before.

Soaring 60 feet into the air, the triangular tower bearing the windmill wheel itself breasted the wind on the hilltop like a storm plow. On the lee side of the tower, a somewhat shorter, octagonal tower seemed to cling to it, as though for comfort. Deep into the earth, like the roots of a tree, went the stone foundations.

"Romeo and Juliet" its designer named it. Its designer, of course, was nephew Frank Lloyd Wright. Romeo and Juliet were to be sheathed in gray shingles. Juliet had a circular staircase and a lookout tower for the children to climb up to. Romeo, of course, did all the work, carrying the wheel and fighting the great southwest winds that periodically swept over the Valley in winter.

The plans were submitted to a builder. The builder said positively the tower would fall down. Aunt Nell was distressed. She said, "I'll telegraph Frank."

"Yes, do," said Aunt Jane. "The poor boy would be so disappointed. I do believe he knows what he's about, even though we don't. Telegraph him, Nell."

Back came the answer: "BUILD IT."

So Cramer, the builder, built it. The aunts purred with delight because it looked so right and pretty. The uncles grumbled because they knew it would fall down, and for years, as storm after storm swept the valley, all five gray-bearded farmers' heads peered disbelievingly out of parlor windows. Romeo and Juliet merely swayed slightly in the wind as Nature and the designer intended. Romeo and Juliet swayed gently to and fro but were never uprooted. Romeo and Juliet stood guard over the farms and the school and the uncles and aunts for 50 years.

It was Frank Lloyd Wright's first real test. For the first

*"The wooden
tower was
rooted as
the trees
are."*

Romeo and
Juliet
Windmill
Tower, 1896

time, "Truth Against the World" had become ṇ.
slogan. It had become a reality. Important to the woṛ.
large? Perhaps not, but to Frank, Romeo and Juliet spoke
with quiet certainty of the kind of faith in himself that he was
always trying to explain to people. He knew it would work,
and it did work. Why wouldn't people listen?

A young publisher, Edward Bok of Philadelphia, did
listen. He also came out to the Midwest, to Chicago and the
surrounding prairie, and he looked. He looked at the general
run-of-the-mill houses, finding them pretentious and uncomfortable. He looked at the Frank Lloyd Wright houses and he
liked them.

The Curtis Publishing Company, of which Bok was the
head, put out a magazine called *Ladies' Home Journal*. Bok
decided that the *Journal* ought to help educate the American
public to the possibilities of this new architecture that he felt
suited American ways much better than the old. So he
launched a campaign. In the first year of the 20th century, a
revolutionary house design appeared in the *Ladies Home
Journal*.

It was called "A Prairie House," and priced at $7,000.
Not more than a few months later a second Prairie House appeared, this one subtitled "A Small House with 'Lots of Room
in It,'" priced at $5,800. The principal features of both
houses embodied most of the ideas their designer, Frank
Lloyd Wright, had been struggling to express ever since his
first design for the Charnley House had actually become brick
and mortar on Astor Street so long ago.

The Prairie House was not fancy. It did not have an
exalted idea of itself. It was planned and scaled to fit the

needs of man and to re-relate man's needs to Nature. A sense of harmony united all elements of the house and the landscape together in a way that had never been done before. Colors, both inside and out, were soft and warm. Browns and buffs and tawny oranges predominated. Textures were no longer smothered by meaningless disguises. Brick emerged as brick; wood did not hide its grain but showed it off; stone was allowed to weather in a natural way.

Chimneys were low and wide, leading to a spacious fireplace in a room which was no longer called the "parlor" but the "living room." The meaning this word "living room" took on in the early 20th century was in itself revolutionary. The old-fashioned "parlor" was a place to entertain special company in. In the parlor, people, balancing teacups, sat around in their best clothes, wiltingly uncomfortable, on horsehair settees or satin and damask upholstered straight-backed armchairs, depending on one's pocketbook.

The parlor was for show. The new living room aimed to become just what it sounded like: a room to live in. It no longer needed the walls of the cardboard box to set up a barrier between it and the neighboring cardboard box, which was usually the dining room.

The Prairie House featured a new sense of space in which interior walls became more like screens or were dispensed with altogether when they were not needed for privacy. And the windows punched in the outside walls had a new look. They were lower, for one thing, as the ceilings were lower, scaled down to suit the size of a man, not a giant. Also, they were longer, sometimes stretching along the whole side of a house, looking out on a garden with a pool, or a hillside, or a stand of trees.

[64]

Altogether a "new look" had come to the Prairie. Not everyone liked it, of course. In fact, in spite of the campaign of the *Ladies Home Journal*, there was a lot of sniffing and snorting on the part of both architects and laymen. "Dress-reform" houses or even "bloomer-houses" was what some people called them, referring, of course, to the kind of revolution advocated in women's clothes. "Temperance houses" said others, referring, of course, to the upsurge of lady prohibitionists who were waging a fierce battle against the devil John Barleycorn.

Enough brave souls in and around Chicago kept the Studio humming with work. Anyone brave enough to build a Frank Lloyd Wright house soon discovered he would also have to be brave enough to live in it. For some reason or other, curiosity-seekers never hesitated about prowling around these strange new structures. Many an early Wright house owner had stories to tell of unknown faces peering in at windows or uninvited visitors turning up at garden parties.

Most early clients of his became friends and submitted themselves, willingly or not, to his adventurous spirit and sometimes tyrannous ways. After all, according to Wright it was only logical that he should have a hand in designing the wardrobe of the lady who was going to live in his house, equally logical that he should choose the furnishings. If there were none available to his liking, what more logical than that he should design these, too?

The results often left something to be desired in the way of comfort. Honorable as his intentions were, he was the first to admit that off and on for most of his life, he was black and blue in one spot or another from the handsome, simple, "comfortable" chairs he himself designed.

[65]

"Repose is the true reward of simplicity."

The Coonley House, Riverside, Illinois, 1908,
the rear from across the pool

Chicago Architectural Photographing Company

Chicago Architectural Photographing Company

The Coonley House living room

"Make all house proportions more liberally human. . . ."

Bone tired, still unable to meet the ever increasing financial burden of his growing family, discouraged by the refusal of his profession to acknowledge him as "one of them," facing a daily fight with contractors and builders who "couldn't or wouldn't" read his plans, Wright was still able to call on his imagination and self-confidence for one last triumph of his early years.

"BUILD IT," he now said to the gentle white-haired Universalist pastor, Dr. Johonnot, who looked up in some alarm from the model of Unity Temple as Frank Lloyd Wright had conceived it. Where was the little white New England church, its tapering spire pointing to Heaven? The pastor was troubled. He wanted to understand the radical structure he saw before him in miniature. Its flat planes, straight lines, the interlocking series of cubes under protruding slab roofs that composed its mass, pleased and thrilled him in a way he had been unprepared for.

Yes, he could sense even from the model that within these walls there was to be a great room. A great room, yes, the exterior walls expressed this. But was it a church? The building committee asked the same question and followed it up with others: Would there be light enough? The lighting was all to be indirect, sifting through concrete beams, filtering through amber glass ceiling fixtures. It was unheard of! "It will be warm as sunlight," Frank said, "and as soft." Could the congregation see the pastor? The pulpit was newfangled. The way people came into the Temple was newfangled. The entrance itself was newfangled. Most of all, the idea of the "room" itself was newfangled. One could see that it had nobility and graciousness. That was true. But—here it came again—the unanswerable question: Was it a church?

[*68*]

The architect who had answers for everything summoned up all his persuasiveness and his convictions and he found he had the answer to this one, too. He remembered, perhaps, the chapel in the Valley and the simple, honest farmers coming from miles around, listening to the words of his preacher uncle. They were not highfalutin words. They were down-to-earth words. The people who listened were down-to-earth people. The religion preached was one of unity. Unity between man and man, between man and Nature, between man and God. A church did not need a spire to point to Heaven to call God down or to take man up. The spirit of God moved in all men, moved in them singly and when they came together in worship and study. The spirit needed no special urging to appear. The pastor listened and agreed. Yes, that was the way he felt about it, and his congregation, he knew, felt the same. This was the feeling he believed in and wanted. He was willing to try.

Unity Temple took two years to build. No contractor wanted to touch it. No building in America had ever been constructed of reinforced concrete poured into wooden frames. It was a gamble. Contractors like to gamble, but only on a sure thing!

To the rescue came Paul Mueller, friend, ally, and experienced builder from the old Adler and Sullivan days. Slowly but surely Unity Temple went up. Its unfamiliar outlines began to take shape under the watchful eyes of Oak Park's "sidewalk superintendents," who gathered month after month, summer and winter, in snow, rain, and sunshine on the corner of Kenilworth and Lake Street to watch the strange goings-on. Often as not, they'd catch a glimpse of the designer himself, a spry and jaunty figure, clambering in and

[69]

around the construction, poking about with his walking stick, stopping to talk with his workmen.

So the building grew, and its "noble room," as Frank called it, officially came to life on a crisp, sunny Sunday in September. Dr. Johonnot, the courageous pastor, preached his first sermon in Unity Temple almost four years after the day he had agreed that the members of his congregation, staunch Universalists, needed no church spire to climb to Heaven on as they met together "FOR THE WORSHIP OF GOD AND THE SERVICE OF MAN".

Unity Temple was—and is today—everything that was hoped for. On that autumn Sunday in 1909, the telephone in Wright's "House with the Tree" had scarcely a moment of silence, as one after another of the pastor's congregation called to congratulate the designer. Finally, the day drew to a close. Frank Lloyd Wright reached for one of his wonderful hats, took his favorite walking-stick from the hall rack, and set out for the autumn woods.

How closely the mood of that autumn afternoon mirrored his own mixed feelings! With what a triumphant flare of color, ranging from the scarlet fire of the sumac to the palest gold of fading maples, summer declared its work was done! But underlying the note of triumph was another note. Was it of sadness? Wright wondered. No, not quite sadness. It was a hint of the coming change, a hint of the new repose gradually settling down upon all growing things. For, if autumn was a time of triumph, it was also a time of withdrawal. Summer's work accomplished, the growing season over and done with, Wright thought he could almost feel nature gathering its forces back into itself, as the long sleep of winter was about to begin. It was time to rest.

". . . the flat plane expressive and always clean cut."

Unity Temple, Oak Park, Illinois, 1906

How badly he needed it too, Wright thought, time to reflect in, time to restore his creative energies, time to rest. He was tired. In Uncle James' words that now came back to him, he had "added tired to tired" until he could go no further. He longed for the repose and refreshment denied no living thing—except, it seemed—a man.

An acorn dropping into the rich leaf mould at his feet promised another spring, a renewal to come, a season to grow in once more. But to Frank Lloyd Wright, twirling his walking stick and watching the smoke of twilight gather in the woods and across the plains on that September afternoon, spring and a renewal of his own life-forces seemed a long way off indeed.

Something had gone out of his work—and out of his life. Something new had crept in: discontent and discouragement. He felt hemmed in, restless, unhappy. The "House in the Tree" had long ceased to give him peace or inspiration. He wished it were not so, but it was. There was nothing to do but face it. Painful as the truth was, he had to face up to it, as always.

The truth was that although the boy's journey of 20 years ago from Madison, Wisconsin to Oak Park, Illinois, was perhaps finally over, the artist's journey was not. Nor was the man's search for what he called "freedom" over. Would it ever be? This was a question he could not answer.

Somehow, somewhere he would have to find freedom. And he would have to go on searching until he did. He knew by this time that freedom was not simply a matter of "inhaling great draughts of space." He knew it was an inner thing he looked for, that no one was going to hand it to him on a silver platter, that his struggle was by no means over.

He knew that the day he left his Oak Park "House with the Tree," society would rise up in arms against him for breaking the rules of conformity in his life as he had broken the rules of tradition in his architecture. Just the same, he would have to go on being himself, being true to the things he believed in.

Well, then, here he was right back to "Truth Against the World." If that was the way he had to take, he would take it, come what might. And he did.

Frank Lloyd Wright's "winter of repose" took him on a two year journey. Paris, Germany, and the ancient Italian hill town of Fiesole sheltered the exile in searcch of freedom— and himself. In 1910, he returned, as was right, natural and altogether predictable, to his beloved Valley, to the hills and wooded ridges of Wisconsin. He returned to build life anew, to make a fresh start. He built a house for himself on the low crown of a hill from which, if he climbed to the very top, he could see Romeo and Juliet sturdy as ever across the way. He called the house Taliesin—Shining Brow. Taliesin was the name of a Welsh poet of ancient times and Frank Lloyd Wright wanted his house to sing as truly as the poet had of his faith in the beauty and the mystery of the natural world, and of man's rightful place within it.

". . . a house that could open to the breezes of summer. . . ."

Taliesin East III, 1925, view from the loggia

Maynard L. Parker

Part Two:

The Sacred Mountain and the Sea

Chapter 8

The Problem of the Catfish

The man who strode vigorously around the deck of the luxury liner *Empress of Russia* gave his fellow passengers the impression of being a tall man, even though he was scarcely more than five foot eight. Also, he gave them the distinct impression that he was "someone," even though they didn't know exactly who he was. His black belted cape billowed out in the sea breeze; he twirled his Malacca cane smartly. His restless eyes swept out across the tranquil reaches of the Pacific, impatient for the first sight of land.

The man, of course, was "someone." He was Frank Lloyd Wright. In his 45th year, Wright was about to face the greatest challenge his career had yet offered him. He was on his way to Japan at the request of the Imperial Government to design and build the new Imperial Hotel in the heart of fast growing Tokyo.

It was 1916. Scarcely a corner of the world had not in one form or another felt the impact of the new century, now well under way. The islands of Japan were no exception.

For more than two hundred years before 1854, the borders of Japan had been closed to foreigners: to new ideas, new ways, new inventions, new forms of government, development of world trade. Closed to the sound of any tongue or the look of any language other than that of the Orient, Japan had lived isolated from the rest of the world through all of the 17th century, the 18th century and half of the 19th century.

But that isolation was over now. In the short span of 50 years since a new and forward-looking Japanese regime had come into power, Japan had begun her dramatic climb from feudalism into the world of today. The story of Commodore Perry's arrival in Yokohama, bearing a letter from President Fillmore to the Emperor of Japan, was history by now. The Japanese in 1853 had been dumbfounded as they watched the ships of the United States Navy steaming into port, black smoke pouring unaccountably from magical funnels, and neither an oar nor a sail to be seen.

The steamship had been only the first of modern marvels to tempt the Japanese out of their ancient ways. The Japanese were a curious people. They had always been quick to learn, and they were unafraid. The feudal code of the Samurai warriors—bravery with honor—ran strong in the hearts of the aristocracy. The newly developed merchant class had welcomed the idea of trade and expansion. The worker in Japan's great rice fields no less than the warrior or the priest, the artist or the craftsman, the philosopher, or the Japanese housewife believed in the divinity of their Empire and their Emperor. For 2,500 years Japan had been ruled by an unbroken line of Emperor gods, descended from Jimmu-Tenno, Japan's first Emperor and great-grandson of the Sun Goddess. Ever since, the Japanese had raised their eyes to the beauty and serenity of snowcapped Fuji, the Sacred Mountain of the Land of the Rising Sun.

No, the Japanese were not afraid of 20th century marvels. Why should they be? Not only were they protected by the divinity of their Emperor, but their island country harbored all kinds of friendly gods devoted to the happiness and well-being of everyday life. One had only to treat these *kami*, as they were called, with reverence and respect and follow the rules laid down by tradition, and all would go well.

The natural world was a kindly world. The gods of the Shinto religion, *kami* of the everlasting rock, the pine tree, the waterfall, the mountain, and the cherry blossom—among a host of others—had much wisdom. So did the spirits of family ancestors, who blessed the simplest Japanese household with their presence.

There was nothing to fear from the modern world, the Japanese decided, and much to learn. They set about learning it as fast as they could. In the past they had absorbed much of the teaching of the ancient world, learning from the Chinese, from the Confucian, the Hindu, the Buddhist and the Brahmin of the East. Now it was the turn of the West to become friend and teacher.

For Frank Lloyd Wright the journey across the Pacific from Taliesin in Wisconsin to Tokyo in Japan was not only a practical journey but a sentimental one. For 16 days as the *Empress of Russia* carried its modern pilgrim farther and farther from the land of automobiles, airplanes, telephones, electric lights, wireless, tractors, refrigerated freight cars, chain stores, radios, Kodaks, canned goods, phonograph records, and rural free delivery, so also it carried him closer and closer to the land of the Ho-o-den Pavilion, of the Kanos, the printmakers, and the philosophers.

Lao-tzu, 500 years before the birth of Christ, seemed to

have summed up Wright's own thinking as well if not better than he could himself. Nature was the great teacher, Lao said. Man had but to learn from her to find true simplicity, contentment, and inspiration.

This was the way of the East. Wright, who had first come to know it and be moved by it in the work of the great Japanese printmakers, now prepared to learn it from life. He was prepared to learn as well as to teach. He knew that although many of the tools and techniques of the Western world might still be wanting in the island empire, traditional ways had a strength and a wisdom all their own.

As Wright took his turns about the deck of the *Empress*, taking in "great draughts" of fresh sea air, he found himself wondering again and again if he could pull it off. Could he really bring the best of the East and the best of the West together, the best of the modern and the best of the ancient ways? This was the artist's question. Wright, the man, put it somewhat differently. On a human level, he found himself asking: Could he bring the Japanese up off the floor where in their daily life they had kneeled for centuries? Could he bring them up to sit on chairs and around a table in a great foyer of the new Imperial Hotel, for instance, without loss of ease or forfeit of dignity in meeting the Western world? Man and artist pondered the answer.

Preliminary plans for the Imperial had been drawn, of course, in the studio-workshop at Taliesin, with icicles dripping off the overhang of the eaves and a log fire burning itself to quiet embers in the deep stone fireplace. The plans had been drawn and approved in the presence of Aisaku Hayashi, manager of the old Imperial, his young wife, Takako-San, reserved and beautiful in her Japanese dress, and the archi-

[*80*]

*"I wanted a home where icicles by invitation
might beautify the eaves."*

Taliesin East III, 1925

tect Yoshitaki. The three had come half way around the world together, looking for someone who could design and build the hotel that Tokyo needed.

The Prairie Houses had impressed them, and so they had sought Wright. And Taliesin had impressed them. It was a new Taliesin. Taliesin II, Wright called it, two years in building, finally completed late in the fall of 1915, a "harmonious house of the North" ready to receive its first three welcome Japanese visitors. Here and there one could see, if one looked hard enough, a hint of the remains of Taliesin I, suddenly and tragically swept to the ground by fire.

Whether or not the Japanese visitors knew of this catastrophe, whether or not something of the love and courage of its builder came through to them as they sat together before the great fireplace, the fact was they loved Frank's house. They found it in no way strange or exotic. On the contrary, it seemed utterly natural to them. They felt at home and at ease in it. They felt at home and at ease with Wright. "It takes me back to Jimmu-Tenno's time," said Hayashi with an air of gratitude and relief.

Wright knew what he meant. Not that Taliesin seemed 2,500 years old, or even that it was in the Japanese "style." Taliesin was neither, of course. What Hayashi meant was that this house had captured the feeling of the North, of wooded hills and rocks and subtle valleys, just as the Prairie Houses seemed to be the natural and logical expression of the plains. Why then, Hayashi was in effect saying, could Wright not enter into and understand the Japanese setting and tradition with equal success?

It was a tribute to Wright, and it was a challenge. Wright needed both badly. It seemed to him as though the

Taliesin fire had wiped out more than a house. Something of Wright's spirit had been trapped in its flames and had died, too. He could and did rebuild the house, but to rebuild one's spirit—that was another matter!

When the official letter of invitation from the Emperor finally arrived, a month or so after Hayashi's visit, Wright had made up his mind. He accepted the commission at once and went as soon as he could, eager, once more, to leave the United States behind for a while, eager for achievement and for recognition.

The old saying, "A prophet is without honor in his own country," seemed bitterly true to Wright. By and large, in spite of the attention he was receiving from European architects, his own American colleagues continued either to ignore or to ridicule his work. He felt, also, that he was personally resented. Some said the Taliesin fire served him right, was just punishment for a rebel, a rule-breaker, an arrogant man. Was he arrogant? Maybe so, he admitted, and added, as though in defense of himself, that in any case it was better to be arrogant and honest than to be humble and hypocritical. If people wanted to confuse his personality with his work, that was their business. He couldn't stop them.

But these bitter memories were safely behind him now, he thought, as the day of arrival approached. He set his heart and his mind on what lay ahead: the greatest challenge he had ever faced. An age-old challenge to every builder in Japan since the beginning of time: earthquake!

The islands of Japan, strung out along more than 1,250 miles of ocean, had been, according to legend, formed by drops of water trickling from the sword of a prehistoric god. According to legend, under the seas of Japan there lived an

[83]

ancient catfish who, not content to slumber forever and ever, now and then flicked his tail restlessly, now and then moved out from under the deep sea rocks where he usually slept, and swam up toward the surface to play. Whenever the earth seemed to sigh beneath them, people said to each other, with a shrug, "Ah, the catfish is waking."

This was the legend. The fact was that periodically the crust of the Japanese Islands, lying truly like the drops of water from a god's sword on the rim of the Pacific, not only sighed but shook, became convulsed by wave after wave of shock from the heaving of the very rocks, deep under the sea's surface, where the legendary catfish was supposed to be taking his legendary nap. In 1703, 1707, 1771, 1855, and 1891, the catfish had wakened.

At least five major earthquakes recorded in little more than 200 years. Each time, thousands of wood and paper houses crumpled to the ground, disappeared into crevasses, or went up in flames with the great waves of fire that invariably followed the convulsive movement of the earth. Each time, thousands of Japanese lost their lives, and nothing could be done about it. Or so it seemed.

The seismograph at the Tokyo Imperial University was never still. Fusakichi Omori, brilliant young professor of seismology, watched, recorded, studied, and warned, pointing out to Tokyo, Yokohama, Kyoto that they were in the active belt and should take steps to minimize the dangers.

What could be done? Build lower? Higher? Of steel? Of wood? What sort of foundations could be sunk to withstand the shocks? Where could they be anchored, and how? To a sea of shifting mud? How guard the water supply? How prepare to fight fire? How? Shrug one's shoulders and trust to fate?

Wright had thought long and hard about the problem. He didn't quite believe there was nothing to be done except to trust to fate and ardently wish repose to the catfish. If an earthquake couldn't be stopped, at least there ought to be a way to survive it, to ride it out. There ought to be a way, he thought, to do exactly this—to *ride* the earthquake out the way a ship rode out a storm at sea. He had the glimmering of an idea. He thought he ought to be able to build the Imperial Hotel so that it *would* ride the earthquake out, not crumple up and disappear in tongues of fire, like a wood and paper house, not crash into a heap of mangled steel, like a skyscraper. The ghost of an idea had come into being on the drafting table, but T square and triangle were not enough. He had to find a way to test it on the soil of the Japanese island where it would ultimately have to sink—or swim.

The ship's anchor dropped in Yokohama Bay. The sails of the sampans were white as birds at rest on the water. Distant, serene, the snowcapped cone of Fuji rose as always, the emblem of Japan, upon the horizon.

Out of the hold of the *Empress* came Wright-o-San's Overland Country Club automobile, and behind the wheel piled Wright-o-San himself. The Japanese adventure, which was to last seven years and to bring both architect and hotel world fame, had begun. The Overland rolled its way cumbrously along the crowded village streets and between the rice fields lying along the road to Tokyo, 25 miles unfolding one after another like a Japanese scroll painting, as though, Wright thought, a Japanese print had come to life.

The catfish, too, soon came to life and stayed lively.

[*85*]

Chapter 9

The Morning Land

From his suite of rooms and workshops in the Annex of the old Imperial Hotel, Wright could look across the square to the Palace grounds. Massive stone walls rose above an ancient moat. Gateways, guarded by blue-tiled, white-walled buildings, opened upon the park within which the ancient Palace stood. Architecture perfect of its kind, Wright thought, and as Japanese as the dark pines that grew in the gardens, as Japanese as the faces of the passersby in the street outside his window.

The new Imperial would have to be as harmonious in its way as was the Imperial Palace, as much a part of the setting as were those dark pine trees, and yet—it would have to have something of Wright's own, of course. Squat and strong, he imagined it, something the Japanese would recognize as having sprung from their own traditions. He began to realize that the plans drawn in the Taliesin workshop were only an architect's exercise, the bare beginnings of an idea. Now, he saw, the new Imperial would have to grow, detail by detail, piece by piece, out of the Japanese ground itself.

He set to work all over again, looking, seeing, thinking, testing, taking stock of the job and of himself. "Form follows function," Sullivan had said, and this credo was never very far from Wright's mind as he began to think out all over again the plans for the new Imperial Hotel.

There was no trouble spelling out what the hotel was wanted for, why the Japanese needed it, and needed it badly. Its first function was to provide comfort for the traveler. Foreigners in vast numbers were beginning to flock to Japan, mostly Westerners who could not live on the floor as the Japanese did, not with grace or ease, and certainly not with comfort. Westerners had to have beds, tables, chairs, and bureaus. They had to have plumbing and modern kitchens, and a lot of other conveniences like they had back home.

Secondly, the Imperial was to be a social clearinghouse, where Japanese officials, businessmen, doctors, lawyers, and bankers could entertain strangers. Very rarely were strangers admitted to the Japanese home or welcomed with Western style hospitality into the intimacy of the family circle. So the Imperial had to serve the purpose of a meeting place. It had to have formal and informal settings. It had to have both ease and elegance; it had to combine the ceremonial with a sense of privacy. It had to do all these things with style.

All architecture, in Wright's view, ought to interpret and reflect the way of life around it and the life to be lived within its walls. The Imperial was no exception. He took a dim view of the skyscrapers imposing their outlines on the Tokyo skyline. Not only were they financially wasteful because all materials had to be imported, but they in no way represented a meeting of the minds between East and West. He would be one foreigner, he decided, to take his hat off to the Japanese culture and to try to learn something from it.

How, for example, did the Japanese live within the walls of their own houses? Wright went out to see, and once more he found his own ideas anticipated by two and a half

[87]

centuries or more. Lao-tzu had said it.

"The reality of the building," said Lao-tzu, "does not consist of walls and roof but in the space within to be lived in." These might have been Wright's words. What did these words mean? However much a house might be what Wright called "thought-built," that is, planned out in the architect's mind with a view to the function it would serve, the landscape it would be a part of, and the people who would live in it, a house ended up by being not an idea or even a blueprint, but a very tangible thing. Architecture had to work.

Well then, what did Lao-tzu's idea mean, if anything, in terms of the Japanese house, Wright asked himself, still groping for the perfect expression of his own ideas.

Cleanliness, simplicity, and a respect for materials were the three cardinal virtues of the humblest of Japanese dwellings. Anything not used was to the Japanese out of place. The "space within" was uncluttered by any objects other than those in immediate use—a low table, cushions on the floor, and in a niche in the wall a painting, a piece of sculpture, or a vase of flowers. Floor mats that served as mattresses were pulled out of cupboards and unrolled on the floor when night came, and in the morning were put away again.

"The European way of arranging a room is, generally speaking, rather revolting to our taste," said a Japanese gentleman delivering himself quietly of these thoughts to a London University audience of the early 1900's. "I have often felt less crowded in a museum or a bazaar than in your drawing rooms." (Well, yes and no! Wright thought, remembering in a moment of nostalgia the orderly disorder of his own vast "drawing-room" at Taliesin.) Certainly, in contrast to the cluttered, gingerbready Victorian mansions he remembered from his youth and early manhood, the cleanness and purity of the Japanese house was as refreshing as the sparkling water of a mountain brook.

Here was something else to learn, he thought. The Japanese used his house with the same naturalness with which a turtle used his shell. The "shell" itself, often of paper and wood, was constructed with mathematical precision according to the size of the house needed. And the size of the house was determined by the number of floor mats, or tatami, needed, each uniformly 3 feet by 6. A Japanese might order a nine, an eleven, a twenty, or a thirty-four mat house much as a Westerner would ask for a two-story house or a three-bedroom apartment or a two-car garage. In Japan, of course, one did not ask for a Tudor house or a Queen Anne cottage or a French chateau. The Japanese house went up with traditional and geometrical grace and logic.

In the truest, simplest sense possible, the size and function of the Japanese two- or four- or sixteen-mat house determined its form, both without and within. Inside, sliding paper screens called shoji, were used at will to divide up the room on the joint lines of the mats. The polished wood posts that carried roof and ceilings also stood at the intersections of the tatami.

Orderly, flexible, and beautiful in its proportions, in its sense of space, and in the softness of light and shadow falling through the paper screens of the partitions, the Japanese house appeared to Wright to be the essence of the "natural house." Everything about it grew logically and naturally. With no waste motion or unnecessary added attractions, the Japanese house grew out of the needs and the innate sense of style of the Japanese.

[89]

The eye found repose, the mind logic, and the body comfort within the four walls, and when the shoji wall screens were moved aside, the world of the Japanese garden offered further proof that man, art, and nature were all of a piece. Everything *belonged*. That was it, and yet, of course, none of it simply "happened."

Wright, seeking to describe what he felt and thought, began to call this "belonging" of architecture to man, to art, and to nature "organic" architecture. In Japan he found it reflected not only in the taste or style sense of one individual or another, but embodied in an entire civilization.

This civilization would change, he knew. In fact, it was in the process of changing, day by day, almost hour by hour. And he was here to help it change, to be a part of Japan's moving into the 20th century and towards the industrialized Western world.

He had been chosen for the job, he reminded himself, because Hayashi believed that he would approach it with the same basic logic, common sense, and philosophy of art—if you could use such a pompous term to describe what Wright himself considered simply "seeing" nature with an artist's eye— that he had brought to the Prairie Houses and to Taliesin. Had Hayashi been right? Would he be able to transpose his thinking, his feeling, and his imagination to the other side of the Pacific? Would his ideas really root and take flower in the Japanese earth? Where to begin?

One began, Wright decided, with the nature of the Japanese earth itself. One began with the fixed fact of earthquakes. There was only one way to approach this fact: with simplicity and directness. The rest, he hoped would follow.

Chapter 10

Something Like a Tree

The year 1916 became the year 1917, and Japanese passers-by began to take for granted the strange machinery that had sprung up out of the earth behind the Annex of the old Imperial Hotel. Nine pile drivers dotted the ground, and around each were clustered a group of 12 Japanese women, singing as they pulled on the ropes that lifted the drive heads until they were high enough to be dropped onto the tapered wooden piles.

Wright-o-San in his broad-brimmed hat, his stalwart American engineer Paul Mueller, and one or another of his 20 Japanese apprentices, architectural students from Tokyo and Kyoto Universities, had also become a natural and normal part of the landscape around the site of Teikoku, the new Imperial Hotel. Hayashi San, the hotel manager, often hovered over the proceedings like a mother hen, and now and then the distinguished Baron Okura made his appearance at the site.

Wright-o-San, it seemed, was testing out his ideas about how to outwit the catfish with the flicking tail. Everyone wished him luck even though what he was doing appeared to be most unorthodox and not a little mysterious. Thousands of small concrete piers began to appear in the ground, none set deeper than eight feet into the cheese-like soil long ago dumped in to fill up the ancient salt marsh on which Teikoku was now to stand. Below the fill was 60 feet of liquid mud, and below that, water, once an arm of Tokyo Bay, separated by no more than 100 miles from Sagami Bay beneath which the catfish slumbered.

An occasional visiting American architect dug his hands into his pockets, shrugged his shoulders, and smiled a knowing smile. The whole operation looked very much like child's play. In a sense, it was. For Wright, with almost childlike directness, had gone straight to the heart of the matter. Studying the patterns of Omori's seismograph, feeling his own bed rock under him at night as though he were back in his cabin on the *Empress*, Wright had decided: why not indeed, float the Imperial on its sea of mud? Buoyant as a battleship on a sea of brine.

With this the goal, the design of the Imperial's foundation supports became all-important. Clearly, they would have to be flexible enough to allow the Imperial to ride out the quake, not rigid enough to anchor her against it. As the first year of trial and error passed, Wright assembled enough data to convince both himself and the inclined-to-be skeptical Paul Mueller that the thousands of shallow concrete piers would do the trick. The foundation would, in fact, float the Imperial, allow her to go with the shock waves and come back, theoretically—at least—unharmed.

All this was highly theoretical, never tried before, unheard of as a method of designing an earthquakeproof structure. Convention had it that either a Japanese house of paper and wood was built and simply laid right down on top of the ground in the usual way, or the builder plunged down 60 feet or more trying to find solid rock to anchor the building to.

And the building was built as solid, as heavy, as rigid, as possible. It was a building that fought back—and, usually, lost the battle.

Once Wright had solved the problem of a flexible foundation, then he began to tackle the problem of the building itself. It would have to be tough, yes, but not heavy, not rigid. Very much to the contrary, it would have to be light and it would have to be flexible, to outwit the quake. Rigidity would never do, Wright figured. No four-square rigid framework could be rigid or staunch enough to withstand the great shock of earthquake. Joints would be bound to snap apart, frames would sag, and the building would crumple under its own great weight.

Lightness was the thing, and that meant hollow masonry, porous rock of some sort, or concrete blocks like Unity Temple. As for flexibility, that was a real puzzler. How could a building hold together and yet yield to movement? How could a building be strong, be tough and yet resilient enough not only to yield to stress but to return to position once the stress and strain had passed by?

Wright locked his hands together in thought and in this very gesture of his own stress and strain, he found the answer. The building would have to be as strong and yet as flexible as the thrust of his own two hands together, fingers locked, able to resist pull yet equally able to return to relaxation and repose. Only steel in combination with concrete could approximate the properties he discovered in his own locked hands. Steel had lightness; it also had this ability to withstand tension, to withstand pull. Within reason an earthquake could push at a building and it would stay together, but pulling on it the quake would tear it apart. The strength of steel under tension made it possible to design a building that would not come apart if a quake pulled at it. The stresses put on a building by an earthquake went every which way, up, down, push, pull. Only steel could give and still withstand, still return, still retain its original strength.

Well, then, he had his problem half solved. The Imperial would float on its flexible foundations. It would be made of light-weight masonry and would be supported by a structure of flexible steel. Still, Wright knew, if he relied on the old-fashioned joint or post and beam construction, his building would go down, no matter how flexible its foundations, how light or resilient its materials. Somehow, he would have to find a way to circumvent the joint, to balance the load of the building in—again—a flexible way rather than supporting it at the usual four corners, each one of which would be a vulnerable point under impact or stress. Rigid corner supports would cancel out any resiliency the Imperial might otherwise have, would detract from any lightness or freedom of design. He would simply be doing another 19th century box.

Why not, then, do away with corner supports altogether? The tensile strength of steel in concrete ought to make it possible to design a structure something like a tree, a central trunk from which the limbs grew out organically on either side, like arms from the body, he thought. With the floors of the building like the arms of the body, no corner supports were needed; the ceilings, in fact, would be suspended from the floors as the drooping fingers of the hand are suspended from the outstretched arm.

This idea, of course, implied the use of the cantilever principle throughout the building, everything supported only at one point like the branches of a tree. The cantilever had never been used before as a central architectural structure in building design. Wright himself had used it often in lesser ways. The flat or low-pitched roofs of the Prairie Houses had hung out over the eaves—cantilevered out, really —balanced on the central support of the house itself. But what he was now proposing to do had never been done before.

Paul Mueller's footsteps resounded on the narrow stairway leading up from Wright's private apartment in the Annex of the old Imperial to the workshop on the roof. Paul seemed tired. It was the end not only of one long day, but of almost a year of long days.

Wright's studio-bed was disordered, as though he had just tumbled out of it and gone straight to the drawing board. He looked as though he had hardly eaten that day. The tray of food on the low table had scarcely been touched. And the drawing board itself! An autumn wind might just have dropped a drift of leaves from a gone summer tree.

"I think it's going to work, Paul," Wright said.

Mueller scratched his balding, sunburned head reflectively and began to pore over the penciled sketches.

"Never been done before," he said finally, echoing Wrights' own thoughts—so Wright said nothing. "On the other hand," said Paul, "I don't know why not. Do you?"

"If a waiter can balance an uplifted tray," Wright said, demonstrating what he meant by bending to the tray of food on the low table, placing it on the palm of one hand, and centering his long, strong fingers under it, then lifting it triumphantly aloft, even waving it to and fro ever so slightly.

"I've seen a native woman carrying a three-foot basket

of laundry on her head," said Paul, not demonstrating but allowing a broad grin to light up his face and crinkle the corners of his eyes.

"Well, then?" Wright's own twinkling eyes were clear as a summer sky.

"What are we waiting for, Wright-o-San?" asked Paul, using the Japanese form of address with affectionate irony. "Remember Unity Temple? They had us on the ropes there too—they thought," he added drily.

"I remember," Wright said, reaching for his Gladstone bag, his stick, his cape, his hat.

Back they all went, back to Taliesin, to the drafting board; students, apprentices, T squares, triangles and, logarithm tables. How much stress could a cantilever bear? Where ought the support to be? How thick? How thin? How tapered? How jointed? How? How? How?

A building 300 by 500 feet, three stories high, to contain 300 bedrooms; to float on a sea of mud; to be light, flexible, tough, strong; to withstand earthquakes.

And to be a work of art, homage to the people of the island of Japan. It was a tall task, indeed, for the Wisconsin son of an itinerant preacher and a Welsh schoolteacher. "The east and the west are mine, the north and the south . . . " sang Whitman.

It was high time, Wright thought, to stretch his muscles again and go to work. He did.

Chapter 11

Baron Okura Calls a Meeting

One thousand and nine days and nights," Wright reckoned it, "I spent building against doomsday."

By the second year, materials and workmen were beginning to be assembled and were flowing into Tokyo from every direction. The site of the Teikoku began to look like a squatter's paradise with the arrival of 600 workmen, mostly with their numerous families, cooking, sleeping, washing— and trying, often in vain, to learn the strange and unfamiliar ways of western building.

Far and wide Frank Lloyd Wright ranged in search of materials to fit his structural needs and at the same time reflect the landscape, colors, textures and forms of Japan. Poking around the hills and valleys, forests and rivers, towns and cities of Japan he went, learning to feel at home in the land of the original Kanos, the land of the bent pine, the black dunes at the side of the sea, the gentle morning light, the rock, the shrine, the waterfall. He explored and recorded what he saw in his mind's eye as he had learned long ago to do when he lay in the tall grass of his uncles' meadows and memorized the sky, the clouds, the shape of the trees, and what made a grasshopper leap across his hand.

The Tokaido, the road from Tokyo to Kyoto, ancient capital of Japan, winding more than 300 miles along the seacoast of Honshu, was famous in art and legend. Naturally, Frank Lloyd Wright had to see for himself the sites immortalized by one of his favorite Japanese printmakers, Hiroshige, in his "Fifty-three Stations of the Tokaido."

Shizuoko, now only a two-hour train ride from modern Tokyo, was one of these stations. Lying deep in a fertile green-tea growing valley, Shizuoko had offered feudal travelers the hazard of three swift rivers that met and crossed each other like serpents. Wright, arriving at Shizuoko, stood on the banks of the rivers and discovered with delight the scene of Hiroshige's portrayal of a man of wealth and power being ferried across the current in his palanquin, carried on the backs of coolies; lesser travellers perched like birds on the strong shoulders of the coolies, whose knowing feet and sturdy legs found their way from one bank to the other.

Wright also now discovered with delight that the Shizuokans were great potters. So he bought a kiln, in which clay from the banks of Hiroshige's river was shaped and fired into long, slim, buffcolored bricks for the outer shell of the new Imperial, and into hollow, fluted bricks for the inside walls.

Two hundred miles north of Tokyo, in the mountainous interior, slumbered the ancient town of Nikko, surrounded by the mouths of old craters and overshadowed by the towering cone of Okushirane volcano. Nikko, like Shizuoka, had had its place in the history and art of Japan. Now it became the scene of art and history-making of quite another kind, for in the great quarry at Oya, Frank Lloyd Wright's search for a suitable material to clothe the Imperial in came to an end. Oya lava in great chunks, greenish and spotted with gold like a tawny leopard, began to join the stream of materials winding their way down to Tokyo.

Pilgrims and vacationers fleeing to Nikko from the hot Tokyo summer, seeking a breath of cool mountain air, lingering by the waterfalls and picnicking under pine trees, worshipping at the Toshogu shrine built in the 17th century at the tomb of the shogun Ieyasu Tokugawa, great fuedal lord and patron of the arts, stayed to marvel at the magnitude of a 20th century operation. For as load after load of Oya lava went down the side of the mountains to the site of the new hotel in Tokyo, deeper and deeper grew the man-made crater left behind. When the sound of the pick against porous rock could be heard no more, and the job was done, the pit could have held the foundations of New York's Grand Central Station. The Japanese shook their heads in disbelief—a very big hole indeed.

Work on the Imperial Hotel grew more and more complicated. Stone choppers—a hundred or more—began to chip away at the chunks of lava, beating out the patterns the face of the building would soon wear. Loads of brick and stone went up and debris went down on the shoulders of the agile Japanese masons who shrugged their shoulders at such unfamiliar laborsaving devices as derricks and hoists.

The services of Endo-San, Wright's Japanese right-hand man, were as often required in interpreting the ways of the West to the ways of the East—and vice versa—as they were required in interpreting the blueprints and elevations of the design. "Give a little here," and "Take a little there," became the order of the day.

Money began to melt away, patience began to wear away, but the building grew and its features began to be recognizable. The shapes of terraces and balconies, of courtyards and pools, began to emerge from the chaos of building materials and workmen's encampments. People began to stand around, sidewalk superintendents no different in a Tokyo Square from those on a Chicago street corner, engaging in

[*99*]

". . . a light, workable lava, called oya. . . .
. . . thin wall shells of slender bricks. . . ."

The Imperial Hotel, Tokyo, 1916-1922

Chicago Architectural Photographing Company

heated arguments with groups of workmen who, as the work progressed, grew more and more eager to explain, defend, and admire the building they had lived with morning, noon and night, for four years now.

The Japanese man on the street had an open mind. He was ready to listen, to look, to learn. Appreciation and loyalty to Wright-o-San and the Teikoku ran strong in the hearts of the small army of masons, coopers, carpenters, hod carriers, roofers, plumbers, students, and foremen. The feeling was catching. Soon no one passed by without a nod or a smile. Encouragement was in the air.

There were exceptions, of course. Certain American architects passing through Tokyo no longer contented themselves with a shrug at the so-called childish follies of one Frank Lloyd Wright. Certain Englishmen unbent themselves enough to gossip about the possible lunacy of an American self-styled "architect," a plainsman from the wilds of far-off Indian-infested country named . . . Wisconsin, was it? or was it Illinois? It didn't much matter. Rumor, as is her way, snowballed, picked up speed like an avalanche until finally the rumor descended full force on the board of directors of the new Imperial Hotel.

Rumor rumbled that Frank Lloyd Wright was mad, that the building would tumble to pieces in an earthquake, and the whole thing sink out of sight into the mud beneath. The sound of the rumble became as unpleasant as a roar in the ears of the members of the board of directors. Because, as it turned out at this crucial moment, 3,500,000 more yen were needed to complete the job.

Baron Kihachiro Okura, chairman of the board, representative of the Imperial Household, financier, scholar, patron of the arts, donator of a museum to the city of Tokyo, collector of Japanese prints, was in his 80's. He had jet black hair and was still fathering a family. He invited Wright-o-San to dinner. It was a ceremonial occasion. It was also a sign of trust and friendship—or so Wright-o-San chose to interpret it.

He was right. The Baron had called a meeting of the board for the following day. His lower lip trembled when he told Wright this, a sure sign of trouble, Wright knew. The Baron was a man of infinite patience. He was also imperturbably polite, as befitted a Japanese gentleman of breeding. "Face" was important. Wright had never seen the Baron lose "face," or lose his temper, either. Only his lower lip stuck out and began to tremble under stress of contained emotion.

Wright was weary, and worried. Also, admire the Japanese as he might, he could not even begin to emulate his host for the evening's extraordinary self-discipline.

Not until dinner was over—an interminable dinner of more than 20 courses consumed on folded knees for hours— had the Baron allowed himself to talk with Wright of the coming battle with the board.

Even then he allowed himself only to say, his lower lip quivering, that the wisdom and loyalty of the representative of the Imperial Royal Household (who was none other than himself, of course) had never been questioned. He allowed himself to add, reassuringly, that he doubted that these virtues would be questioned now. Furthermore, it was in the best interests of the Imperial Royal Household—he did *not* allow himself to pronounce the name of the Emperor—that Teikoku fulfill its promise, and that the "young man" be permitted to complete his job.

[*102*]

"All things are relative," said Wright to himself, bowing and bidding the Baron good-night. A mere lad, a stripling, he might appear to this venerable octogenerian who accepted with a gracious nod Wright's assurance that he would, indeed, complete his job and the hotel would, indeed, fulfill its promise. The fact was that Wright did not feel in the least like a lad. He was 51 years old and he felt all of his 51 years, particularly at this moment in his knee joints!

Back in his own apartment at last, he lit a fire in the small living-room fireplace, slipped out of the ceremonial kimono he had donned for the Baron's dinner, got into his working clothes and—after a moment's hesitation because of the lateness of the hour—decided to send for Endo-San. Perhaps together they might find a way they hadn't yet thought of, a shortcut. Three and a half million yen had an astronomical sound, even to Wright's ears. Had they made mistakes? If so, where?

Waiting for Endo-San, Wright found himself wondering what trick of fate, or act of God, or will of man, or accidental turning point in his life had brought him here. What a far cry from a platter of corn-beef hash in Kinsley's restaurant wolfed-down hungrily by a country boy barely arrived in bustling Chicago to a 20-course ceremonial dinner, followed by an equally ceremonial tea-drinking in the home of a Japanese aristocrat!

Wright was homesick.

An unanswered pile of mail nagged at his conscience. Word had somehow got to his mother that he wasn't well. It was true. The Pacific lowlands of Japan, hot and humid in summer and penetratingly damp in winter, had depleted the energies of the Northerner used to a briskness in the air and the occasional smell of snow. She wanted to come over and see to her son, his mother wrote. She was over 80. He had to find time to write and tell her: "No, don't come!"

From California came disturbing news of the houses in progress there. In the architect's absence, contractors misread plans, by-passed specifications. Temperamental clients suffered from mounting doubts and anxieties, were advised and counter-advised by well-meaning friends. Things got to be a muddle. He could not be in two places at once. A letter, at least . . . Wright sighed.

From Chicago, furthest away of all, and nearest in a sense to his heart, an unopened letter awaited him. He didn't believe in premonitions. Yet why had he allowed it to lie unopened on the desk? It had been there waiting for him when he came in from the day's work. It continued to wait, unopened, while he allowed his Japanese houseboy to soap and rinse away the day's grime from his aching body before he sank gratefully into the deep wooden tub of steaming water. It continued to wait while he outfitted himself in his silk ceremonial kimona, white tabi-socks, and wooden clogs; while he went out to dinner; while he ate; while he returned.

It still awaited him. He went over to the desk and opened it. Louis Sullivan, lonely, ill, bankrupt, ignored by all but a few of his oldest friends and associates, wrote with eloquence of the pride he took in what Wright was doing.

"You are possessed of a rare sense of the human and an equally rare sense of Mother Earth. Never mind those who cling for safety to old ideas, superstitions and taboos. The idea of freedom is older than the slave idea," wrote Louis Sullivan.

[104]

" 'Crank,' 'visionary,' 'dreamer,' 'freak,' I have known you since you were eighteen years old. Hold tenaciously to the single thought. It is an epic poem you are addressing to the Japanese people."

Well, he thought, the letter in his hand and now his hand doubled into a fist, he had his answer. The courage to go on! Perhaps he had made mistakes, costly ones even, in the name—ironically—of economy: such as abolishing the expensive covershed under which most buildings were built in Japan only to discover that the Japanese knew their climate better than he did. Came the rainy season. The Japanese said it rained from the ground up as well as from the sky down. It did, Wright discovered. Then came the burning midsummer sun. The air was humid as a steam bath.

Wiping the sweat out of his eyes, the architect was the first to admit his face was red—red with humiliation as well as with the heat. Seven months, at the very least, were lost in this costly effort to economize. American efficiency and the Japanese climate were poles apart. The courteous Japanese only smiled, and no one said, "I told you so." No one had to!

Wright set his lips grimly together. "Hold tenaciously to the single thought!" Sullivan was right, of course.

Yes, even though he had made mistakes, even though the work had now and then ground slowly to a halt for one reason or another, in spite of this the job was two-thirds finished. It was no time to compromise. Wright never had. Why begin now?

Never mind the "fashionable epithets," wrote Sullivan. "Freak, dreamer, visionary, eccentric!" How fashionable was the epithet "Madman!" Wright wondered, smiling to himself in the stillness of the Tokyo night as he thought of tomorrow's meeting. With the dignified presence of the Baron at the head of the table, would the word "madman" actually be uttered aloud? and if so, by whom? White-haired Asano-San, giant of the shipping interests? Mild-voiced tobacco tycoon Murai? Banker Wakai, broad as he was long, whose august beard reached to the hem of his kimono? Would any of them dare?

What difference would it make if they did! There could be no giving in, no giving up! The Emperor of Japan wanted his Teikoku as it had been promised him. Well then, he should have it. He *would* have it, and the people of Japan would have a haven of safety against the catfish.

Wright's fatigue vanished. He felt as refreshed as if he had had a long night's dreamless sleep. He had met doubts before, scorn, ridicule, even muttered questions of his sanity. Lieber Meister had met the same doubts before him, yet Lieber Meister would never give up. Why should Frank Lloyd Wright? Was he a lesser man? Lieber Meister never flinched from truth, or deviated from courage. "Lieber Meister still had something to teach his student, it seemed!

The Tokyo night wore on, and the years seemed to dissolve away in a gentle curtain of falling rain from that long ago afternoon when a tempestuously angry young Frank Lloyd Wright had strode out of Sullivan's office and slammed the door. The years dissolved away, as a full-fledged architect now sat down at a desk overlooking a Japanese garden to write a letter.

"Dear Lieber Meister," he began. His rapid hand covered page after page with the tale of his Japanese experience. He wasted little time with details of the attacks against him. After all, what did they matter? When had the littleness of small minds ever mattered? People only saw what they were

[*106*]

capable of seeing, usually the so-called "facts," and people were limited in their perception of what they considered "facts" by what other people had already thought or said or done before about them.

Go one step further, as Wright did. Take the facts, not as they were *considered* to be but as they really were, let intuition go to work and commonsense and imagination, and someone, more often a lot of someones, would begin to yank on the reins and loudly call, "Whoa! where are you going?"

"It is the easiest thing in the world," Wright wrote, "to get hit by 'facts'—and to miss the truth. It takes something of a poet to understand that a 'fact' is not necessarily the truth!"

The Japanese printmakers, for instance, understood that, he wrote. The Japanese artist was a poet—with a brush for a pen. With the rare gift of understatement and no waste motion, the print went right to the heart of the matter, illuminating the "fact," yes—but the poetic truth that gave it life even more so.

"The print is more autobiographical than you may imagine. *Everything insignificant has been eliminated* from it. As you say of me that I have reduced thinking to 'simples', so with the print. It is like a window through which I look upon my own work. And so there is always the quest for the Japanese print, and the mysterious, wonderful, ancient Tokyo called "Yeddo" to explore. A byroad by which I see. . ."

Festooned with red paper lanterns, crowned with gay temples, the seven hills of ancient Yeddo cradled a teeming city. Along the bare earth streets, in and out of the labyrinth of highways and byways, gaudy ghosts of centuries past stepped as though from the palette of a Hiroshige, a Harunobu, a

Hokusai, jostling the wandering American.

Sometimes the American was alone, sometimes with friends. He did not lack for companionship—if he wanted it. There was Motoko Hani, the independent, forward-looking Japanese founder of Jiyu Gakuen Girls School, which she called the "School of the Free Spirit." Frank Lloyd Wright's design for the new classroom and dormitory buildings pleased her enormously. Sometimes it was Hayashi-san who, at the end of a long day's work, joined Wright in his enchanted forays into the maze of old Yeddo streets. Sometimes it was Wright's oldest son, John, an architect in his own right by now, come to Japan to help his father oversee the growth of the new Imperial, who strode along at Wright's side, towering over the crowds on the avenues on a Saturday afternoon. Or it might be the Baron Okura himself, who on a rare occasion accompanied his client in his pursuit of the elusive Japanese print. Okura's own taste and judgment were unerring; Wright's not always so. Wright's enthusiasm sometimes got the better of his expert knowledge. All the same, his collection grew and his knowledge and love along with it.

Behind the luminous screens of houses lining the quiet streets, Wright sensed the family circle within. He imagined he heard—and perhaps he did hear—the soft padding of white tabied feet over polished floor and rustling tatami. Lengthening his own steps on the clean swept, bare earth, nearly empty avenues, swinging his cane, listening and looking to the night sounds and the night sights of Tokyo, he remembered the night streets of another city—Chicago. How remote they were! And in memory even uglier, drearier, bleaker than any city streets anywhere had a right to be.

Cities bred inhumanity, he thought. What, he asked,

would happen to ancient Yeddo after a generation or so of industrialization had gone by? In his own land, man had not yet learned to master the machine, to use it for his own best interests, to make it an ally in the search for truth and beauty. The city ground people down like a machine and spewed them all out again in the same mold, ground down individuality, spewed out grayness. The city closed out the sky and frowned on a blade of grass. Would the same thing happen here?

Over the garden wall, the passerby might catch a glimpse a group of elderly Japanese gentlemen proceeding with dignity down a scrap of winding path to a thatch-roofed tea cottage in the moonlight. This was the old Japan. Would the new Japan forget that the occasion of a full moon or the early flowering of the plum branch or a fresh snowfall over the cone of Fuji was of sufficient importance to call for a meeting of the minds over the ceremony of brewing and pouring and sipping tea? Would the roar of traffic drown out the sound of the old men's voices as they told each other how it used to be when the wind whistled through the pine trees of their youth?

The embers in the little fireplace grew gray with the dawn. Wright, turning from his desk with a little shiver of cold, saw that Endo-San had fallen asleep, stretched out on the floor in the Japanese manner with his hands folded under the nape of his neck.

Wright thought he must have fallen asleep, too. For how long, he did not know. He did not remember hearing Endo-San come into the room. For a moment, dazed, Wright even forgot why he had sent for him in the first place.

Then he did remember—all too well! The board of directors' meeting was only a few hours away. Ought he to rouse his assistant? Go over the facts and figures with him once more? As though they hadn't already done this time and again, poring over the specifications, the costs, the future needs. No, let Endo-San sleep.

The smell of rain was still in the air and the little garden below was wet with mist. But, save for a wisp of fog on the horizon, the slowly brightening sky was cloudless. Soon the Japanese houseboy would come to brew and serve the mornign tea, and the work day would begin. Wright turned back to his desk.

"In the morning land," he concluded his letter to Lieber Meister, "I found this simple everyday singing of the human spirit—a 'song to heaven'—I am calling it—to be the everyday dwelling place of the Japanese people. The Japanese lavish loving care on their beautiful things. To them beautiful things are religious things and their care is a great privilege. We of the West couldn't live in Japanese houses and we shouldn't. But we could live in houses disciplined by an ideal at least as high. . . .

"Your ideals have been at least as high, old master," he whispered, sealing the letter. "Let mine fall no lower!"

Endo-San stirred and sat up, abruptly awake.

"And now," said Wright partly to his assistant and partly to the watery sun rising wanly over the garden well, "let's get on with the job."

"Shibui," said Endo-San smiling and springing to his feet.

"The reward for earnest contemplation?" Wright said, a little unsure of his ground.

"That is right," said Endo-San.

"And what is the reward?"

"The new day!" said Endo-San.

"May it bring us luck," said Wright grimly.

"May it smile on us," said Endo-San.

Was it a coincidence that at that precise moment the catfish chose to flick his tail? Ever so gently, to be sure. The temblor came and went in a matter of seconds. The two men looked at each other, needing no words to express the thoughts that flashed simultaneously into both men's minds: *Time was running out!*

. There had been ample warning that the quake was about to strike again. That morning, Fusakichi Omori, at his seismograph as always, noted the shock, the third in a week. For years he had been patiently recording and plotting all the movements of the earth's crust—the after-shocks of the last great earthquake to strike Japan. Also he had studied all available records of the series of fore-shocks preceding that October day in 1891 when 7,279 Japanese lives were lost, 17,393 injured, more than 200,000 houses destroyed in whole or in part, by the quake itself, or by the devastating fire that followed.

Professor Akitsune Imamura had also put himself on record, more than ten years before that morning when Frank Lloyd Wright and Endo-San felt the floor of the Annex move under their feet and watched the surface of the amber tea in the teacups appear to slide back and forth. Unless Tokyo improved her water supply and fire protection, Imamura had warned in the Japanese journal *Taiyo*, a new quake would cost more than 100,000 lives—and a new quake, he feared, was on the way.

When would it hit? Would it be the last of the aftershocks of 1891, as Omori believed? Or were these weekly temblors the fore-shocks of a new quake? No one knew. There was no way of telling.

The houseboy set the tea-tray down and shrugged his shoulders. "*Shikata-gai-nai*": It cannot be helped.

The grim silence with which the meeting of the board of directors began did not last long. Soon the mutterings began and the talking, all at once, from everyone, on every side. Except for the Baron, who held his peace—for a while! Suddenly, it appeared, he had had enough of the querulous, angry, whining, insistent, belaboring of his colleages—about the foundations, the foundations, the foundations; the money, the money, the money. It was too much for the Baron. The honor not only of the "young" architect was at stake, but of the representative of the Imperial Household.

The Baron rose. Both fists pounded on the table. Hissing with anger, he called for silence. He got it. He turned to the architect, sitting with his interpreter at the other end of the table.

Wright found himself getting to his feet, too. In rapid-fire Japanese, the Baron spoke his piece, short and to the point.

Politely, the interpreter, also on his feet by now, translated: "If the architect would remain at his post until the job was completed, the Baron himself would find the necessary money and the directors could go to the devil!"—or wherever it was, Wright thought, that the Japanese went to in a case like that!

It was all over. Inwardly shaking with fatigue and illness, Wright held out his hand. The Baron clasped it. The compact was made.

Chapter 2

"Banzai, Wright-o-San"

A year to go! In April the cherry-blossoms appeared and all Japan turned out to see. In the blue waters of Lake Kawaguchi, the snow cone of Fuji mirrored itself as though crowned with the symbol of springs, its image wreathed with the sprays of the blooming cherry that had burst into delicate flower in the warm sunlight along the shores of the lake.

In June, the Emperor celebrated his birthday in the traditional fashion with a garden party. And in June, the Emperor—and Frank Lloyd Wright—had an unexpected guest.

Anna Wright, who had never been stopped before in her life when there was anything she had set her mind to do, was not to be stopped now by a matter of mere years. Eighty of them, to be sure, but she had heard that the Japanese venerated old age, and she wanted to find out for herself. Also, of course, she wanted to have a look at Frank.

She did both, and she found both greatly to her liking. The Japanese adored her. At the Emperor's garden party, everyone said Anna Wright looked like a queen. She went everywhere with Frank's friends, saw everything, and had no lonely hours even though Frank himself could find little time to spare in those last hectic months of work.

Work never hurt anyone, thought Anna Wright, least of

all a Lloyd-Jones. Frank was thinner, a little on the tense side; but then he had a right to be, she thought. The Lloyd-Joneses were hard to beat. Frank would come out on top. They all did. She couldn't understand why people thought it was heroic of her to get herself aboard a steamship and cross miles of ocean to see for herself what was happening in Tokyo.

She hadn't the least doubt that Frank would get his hotel built in spite of all the skepticism and suspicion he was surrounded by, in spite of the sly whispers that she heard perfectly well but held her head high, affecting not to. He would get it built and it would stand up—to anything. Like Romeo and Juliet, still standing guard over the farms in her Wisconsin Valley, storms or no storms.

Anna Wright, after all these years, was beginning to get used to the storm clouds that periodically gathered about her son Frank. Sometimes they broke and sometimes they didn't. Whether they broke or not, Frank could weather them, she knew. She went home, secure in the knowledge that her dreams had not failed her. Frank was an architect, as all the world would soon be bound to see.

There was still suspicion, yes, and skepticism, and still the sly whispers and the black looks on the faces of the directors. Even the Baron came near to giving in as the months passed by—and as the bills mounted.

Forty-thousand yen to build a pool? Why not economize here? Who ever heard of an enormous useless pool right in the entrance court of a hotel building? Flanked by terraces and overhanging gardens from the cantilevered roofs above, it might be a pretty sight indeed, and a refreshing one to the hot and weary traveller. But who needed it? "Eliminate the pool," said the Baron. It was clear his mind was made up.

This time it was the architect who was patient, who was polite—and who was firm. "The pool is the last resource against the quake," explained Wright. The interpreter's eyes lit up for a fraction of a second. He translated, turning with courteous impassivity to the Baron.

"I know," said the Baron. "Eliminate it."

"If disaster strikes, city water will be cut off," said Wright.

The Baron nodded and did not look up from his desk.

"Even though the piping of Teikoku is designed to withstand shock, of what value will that be if the city water is cut off? if the city mains go? There will be water only in the pool. No other water to fight fire with. The pool is a reservoir."

"Tell him," said the Baron to the interpreter, "I will listen to no further arguments. I know them all." The interpreter complied. "Eliminate the pool," concluded the Baron.

"Tell him," said Frank Lloyd Wright, "that if the pool goes, I go. He will have released me from our bargain."

The Baron stood up in silence. His lip trembled He bowed. The interpreter bowed. Frank Lloyd Wright bowed— and left the office. There was nothing more to say. The pool stayed.

Work never faltered, and the seismograph was never still. "About to sleep," wrote Frank Lloyd Wright, "the bed seems to disappear under you. Awakened at night by strange sensations—sudden shocks, upheavals and swinging. Jolting back and swinging. There may be a more awful threat to human life than earthquake. I do not know what it can be. The terror of the temblor never leaves me. . . ."

At last Teikoku was nearing completion. All but one wing of the hotel was not only up but furnished. Rugs especially woven to harmonize with the warm colors of the interiors had arrived from Pekin. Sunken bathtubs of mosaic in soft ivory-colored stone had been set in place. Cork lined the floors of the corridors. Sills of waxed Hokkaido oak glowed warmly in the subdued light of indirect fixtures.

From the tiled balconies or the terraces outside each suite, one could look down upon the complex of gardens and the pool where water lilies were soon to be planted. Gigantic though the Imperial was, nowhere was the sense of size oppressive. No, the Imperial was certainly not a great marble temple on a hill to be marveled at. Nor did it look like a monolithic warehouse subdivided into little cells like a beehive. It did not tower above the Tokyo skyline. It did not strut with the sleek pride of unblemished modernism—there were no bright steel or bone-white concrete surfaces to turn a brash modern face to the Emperor's Palace across the way. The hand-hewn lava, the turquoise copper roof trim, the planted concrete terraces, the vistas from every window and at the turn of every corridor were full of the mystery, of the privacy, of the brooding quiet that Wright had found in the winding streets of ancient Yeddo. The new Imperial was scaled to the size of a man, and to the intimacy of the Japanese landscape. If the the Japanese were going to have to get up off their folded knees to greet their Western colleagues, there was no reason for them to give up, in the process, the soft-spoken, quiet, intimate relationships so much a part of their everyday lives.

As for Wright's own Western colleagues, let them criticize him for "abandoning modernism" as they had once criticized him for "abandoning classicism." He was prepared!

Allowing himself a rare moment of daydreaming, as he leaned his elbows on the sill of the casement window in his new office overlooking the entrance court of Teikoku and watched the workmen spading new earth into the planters by the side of the pool, Wright was *not* prepared for the panic that struck all of Tokyo a second or two later, a second before the stroke of noon, Wednesday, April 26, 1922.

Drawing boards and draftsmen went sprawling to the office floor without warning as a gigantic jolt lifted the whole building and shook it like a bone in the mouth of an angry dog. A moment later the earth waves began.

Knocked down by the rush of workmen running for their lives, Wright lay on the floor and waited. A long timeless moment with no end, it seemed! He could actually see the ground swell heaving its way through the construction above with hideous crushing noises. Grinding and groaning, and several thunderous crashes reached his ears. Was it the banquet hall?

His eyes met those of Endo-San. Endo-San, prone on the floor, white-lipped and perspiring, waited too. Utter silence followed. Except for them, the building was deserted.

Then bells began to ring and the sounds of weeping and wailing women came from the streets below. Shaking, Frank Lloyd Wright and Endo-San went out together on the roof to see. Fire had broken out in a dozen places. Across the street stood a strangely silent crowd of workmen staring in disbelief at the two men on the roof of Teikoku. Next door was a gigantic heap of rubble, a tumbled pile of brick and mortar— all that was left of the five tall chimneys of the old Imperial.

[*117*]

Those thunderous crashes, then, had not been the banquet hall. Teikoku had come through undamaged.

Wright and Endo-San managed a smile and a wave to the shaken workmen across the street. Up went a shout: "Awright! Sayonara! Banzai. . .Wright-o-San."

Professor Fusakichi Omori picked himself up off the floor of his office in the Seismological Institute of Tokyo Imperial University. He ought—at that moment, shortly after the stroke of noon—to have been on his way home for lunch, but he had been unusually busy that morning with student conferences and an unscheduled visit from a worried city official. The frequency and severity of the shocks seemed to have increased over the last weeks. At least, some of the younger men in Tokyo's official and semi-official positions of responsibility were not entirely satisfied* with the time-honored *Shikata-gai-nai* attitude toward future quakes. Omori's accumulated data indicated that precautions certainly ought to be taken against a severe shock coming somewhere in the Tokyo vicinity, and soon. In the immediate future, Omori had stated with grave concern.

Omori dusted himself off. He was, unaccountably, shaking. It seemed, for a moment, as though he himself had summoned the shock—by forecasting it only that morning. No, that was absurd superstition! Omori's scientific mind righted itself instantly, and with a sense of realistic alarm, now he hurried down the corridor, opened the steel door at the end of it, and made his way down the spiral staircase into the fireproof underground vault where the seismograph was installed. This much, he hoped, at least they had learned from the Mino-Owari quake of 1891, in which the seismograph itself had been buried in the debris of its shelter so that it

[*118*]

took seven hours to restore it to working condition. They had learned, he hoped, to protect their precious instruments from disaster. Or—had the instrument once again failed?

No, it had not! With carefully disciplined fingers, Omori mastered his impatient desire to know the worst at once. Patiently he removed the strip of graph paper from its drum. There it was! No possible doubt about it! Tokyo had suffered the worst shock of years! Patiently, carefully, Omori once more studied his assembled data. He drew a reasonable and well substantiated conclusion, and he made his prediction. This was what Omori said:

That the shock of April 26, 1922 was the principal shock of the series of tremors that had been plaguing Tokyo since Mino-Owari; that it would be probably the last for some time to come; that Tokyo, in short, ought not to have to worry about major earthquakes for a century or more.

Everyone heaved a vast sigh of relief, including Omori himself, of course. Including Frank Lloyd Wright.

Frank Lloyd Wright's task was over. The 1001 days and nights of the Tokyo adventure had come to an end. The Imperial had ridden out the quake as the architect had predicted she would. The foundations—ah, yes, those foundations!—showed no deviation whatsoever. Frank Lloyd Wright could go home now, and he did, sailing away from Yokohama. The farewell shouts of his workmen rang in his ears.

The shoreline, abrupt and mountainous; the terraced hillsides; the straw-thatched villages; the white-sailed sampans; the distant cone of the Sacred Mountain faded from view, as Frank Lloyd Wright looked for the last time on the "morning land." Both were serene in the knowledge that they

[119]

had come through. And that the catfish would not trouble to strike again—for a while, at least!

But the science of seismology was as young as the catfish was old. Or, to put it another way, Professor Fusakichi Omori got hit by "facts"—and missed the truth. For, two years later, again as the midday sun rode high in the cloudless sky over Tokyo, one minute and twenty-eight seconds before noon on September 1, 1923, the thin crust of earth under Sagami Bay snapped. The earthborne waves of shock rolled outwards and onwards; and in a matter of seconds, death and destruction had visited 90 miles of Japanese coastline, devastating Yokohama and sweeping on down to Tokyo.

Half an hour later, over 100 fires had broken out in the city. Two and half days later, when the last of the flames had flickered and gone out, thousands found themselves homeless. More than 350,000 houses had flickered and gone out, too. The dead, the missing, the injured numbered in the hundreds of thousands. The stricken area began numbly to take stock of what had happened. It was the worst natural disaster the modern world had ever seen. *Shikata-gai-nai?* Perhaps. . .

The science of seismology grew up overnight and issued a new warning. *Never predict anything about earthquakes!*

Chapter 13

Home to Taliesin

The next two years passed by almost like a mirage in the planted desert of Southern California. Surrounded by the Hollywood hills, golden brown in the sunlight and spotted like the skin of a leopard with patches of grease bush and sage, Wright still dreamed of the 1001 days and nights in Tokyo, of IMPEHO, as the new Imperial was now known.

But California had work to be done, and Wright was there to do it—if he could. The familiar battle began again, the wearisome struggle against the deceit and ineptitude of contractors, the shoddiness of workmanship, the disenchanting advice of well-meaning friends, and the ravages of a climate that baked an unsuspecting house roof to a crisp most of the year and then drenched it the rest of the time.

Just the same, in those two years, two houses did get built, and others began to take shape on the drawing board. Wright's second architect-son Lloyd was on hand to help. His clients stood by. What else could a man want?

Taliesin, of course! The house of the north had languished in its owner's absence long enough. It was time to go home. High time! Fall was in the air of the beloved Valley, and only one faithful apprentice, a couple of caretakers, and the nameless ghosts of the ancient Druid gods asleep on the rock ledges under the crisp and starry autumn sky were there to listen for the whisper of the wind and the rustle of leaves, to watch for the battalions of honking geese winging their way south once more from the wilderness of the north.

At last the work was done. Hollyhock House and La Miniatura, the one high up on Olive Hill in splendid isolation, the other deep in an intimate ravine, set among filigreed, tattered eucalyptus trees reflected in a quiet pool, came near to setting a new style in the oasis of the Southern California desert. They did not look like houses transplanted from the Midwest, complete with porches, rocking chairs, and pitchers of ice water. Nor did they look like the Missions of Fra Junipero Serrra or San Juan Capistrano, copied freely up and down the California coastline and called "Spanish."

Wright ignored both "styles." He looked at the dramatic nature of the land itself, a land wrenched upwards in a series of violently rising hills and tangled canyons from the rim of the Pacific to the edge of the sky; a land which fell away again to a sunbaked valley that carried more than a hint of the arid desert it once had been. He turned his back on small "lots" and on the little plastered caverns of houses that passed for architecture. He turned his back once more on an artiness that passed for art.

Hollyhock House and La Miniatura met the drama of the landscape with a drama of their own. Both were experimental in design. Some said they looked like Mayan temples or, predicting disaster as usual, said they would soon look like Mayan ruins. Both were experimental in structure—no one had thought of using the lowly materials of poured concrete or the textured concrete block in house construction. These were the gutter-rats of the building materials. Gas stations, yes. Houses, well hardly! Hollyhock House and La Miniatura won the battle against conformity hands down. But the architect himself had had enough. He was more than ready to remove himself from the struggle to achieve quality in a community that valued the ability to "get by." Everyone was out to "get by" or to "sell something." He didn't want to get by or to sell anything, least of all himself. He didn't like being a commodity for sale. "One architect knocked down to the highest bidder" was how he began to feel in sunny Southern California. Other things irked him, too. The press, for instance, was one of the things he didn't take to very kindly. Nor they to him. Not that he had ever been very fond of the newspaper "boys" anywhere, he would have to admit. They were always in at the kill, whenever there was a kill or even the smell of one.

On September 1, 1923, news of the Tokyo disaster swept the nation and the smell of the kill was in the air for sure! At two o'clock in the morning the call from the Los Angeles *Examiner* came in. "They" had the honor of informing Mr. Wright that the Imperial Hotel was a shambles. Yes sir, completely destroyed, razed to the ground if not buried beneath it. Had he anything to say?

Indeed he did; he had plenty to say.

"Wait," he said. "Every other public building in Tokyo is called the Imperial. The Imperial Theatre, the Imperial Hospital, the Imperial This, and the Imperial That. Wait and see," he said. "The Imperial Hotel will be above the ground if anything is." They laughed.

"You will have to retract," he said. "If you print now, you will have to retract later."

Sorry, they said. We will have to print now.

[*123*]

Ten agonizing days and nights went by. Was it true? Had the catfish won? Would Okura, Hayashi, Endo-San—all his Japanese friends and faithful allies—be left shrugging their shoulders and saying in the fashion of centuries: *Shikata-gai-nai!* If, that is, they were alive to say anything at all. Reports of the toll of the dead and missing rose daily.

Then from Wright's Los Angeles studio on Olive Hill the news flashed around the world. This is the way the *real* news read:

13 Sept. 1923

FRANK LLOYD WRIGHT
OLIVE HILL STUDIO RESIDENCE B 1645 VERMONT
AVE HOLLYWOOD CALIF FOLLOWING WIRELESS
RECEIVED FROM TOKIO TODAY HOTEL STANDS
UNDAMAGED AS MONUMENT OF YOUR GENIUS
HUNDREDS OF HOMELESS PROVIDED BY PER-
FECTLY MAINTAINED SERVICE CONGRATULA-
TIONS SIGNED OKURA: IMPEHO

Frank Lloyd Wright packed up his belongings and said goodbye to Southern California. With Okura's wire in his pocket, he climbed aboard a sleeper in Los Angeles' Spanish type mission Terminal. No crowd of cheering workmen was there with Banzai's, laughter, and tears as there had been in the harbor of Yokohama two years before.

Never mind, IMPEHO had come through, and so had he! Now he was hungry for more news. Perhaps it would be waiting for him on the great table in his workshop at Taliesin. He was impatient now, impatient for the scent of the Wisconsin woods and the Wisconsin earth, impatient for the first sight of the beloved valley he had left too long behind.

Like a great sleek beast of the night, the train slipped

[*124*]

away from the lights of the city, mounted the encircling foot-hills, and slid away across the dark floor of the desert, heading eastward at last. Heading for home.

There was news. Endo-San wrote:

"First came the shock without any previous signs of any kind. Rolled out of the house and ran to Imperial rear court. The ground there cracked and moved just like waves, and water sprang along the crevices; couldn't hold myself upright: watched the building; it shook like a little toy. Down came the restaurant across the street in the park and fire broke out the next moment. Taisko Kaikas restaurant . . . roof flat on the ground.

"Horror-stricken people running to and fro, women weeping like little children.

"Four stone figures fell, two along pool sinking into ground as though nothing had been there before.

"Front hall—nothing. Perforated lanterns on piers peaceful as ever.

"Dining room—no damage.

"Theatre—nothing noticeable.

"Banquet hall—as glorious as ever.

"Slam-bang business came again. On banquet floor forty feet high above ground. Came with such horrible roar swept me off my feet to floor; tottering and uneasy came to post, and sustained myself, and watched.

"So the Imperial has come through this test and she stands like the sun . . ."

The Baron wrote:

"Both great Tokyo homes are gone. The Museum and its contents destroyed. The Imperial stands . . .

"The Japanese coming in droves dragging their children

into the courts and on to the terraces of the building, praying for protection by the God that has protected that building.

". . . as the wall of fire, driving a great wail of human misery before it, came sweeping toward the long front of building, hotel boys formed bucket line to the big pool, the water there the only water available anywhere . . . kept the window sashes and frames wet to meet the flames that came leaping across the narrow street."

A stranger wrote:

"My friend, after first quake, thought only of his wife and child in the Imperial Hotel, which he being influenced by the comment he had so often heard thought would be one mass of ruins.

"His surprise was as complete as his happiness."

Another unknown friend:

". . . in the basement office, my secretary, Miss Satterthwaite was at work at time of earthquake. Not a glass was broken and 10 minutes after shock she returned to work."

Poor Miss Satterthwaite, thought Wright. He would have offered her his profound apologies if he could. Again midway between tears and laughter—who could he share them with, either the tears or the laughter?—he dug once more into the pile of unopened letters, telegrams, newspaper clippings, requests for interviews, for articles—the *Forum*, the *Record*, *Liberty* magazine. In vain he searched the haystack for one needle. The American Institute of Architects, the A.I.A.! Could they still fail to recognize him? They had predicted disaster for IMPEHO. Would they not now acknowledge their mistake?

No, they would not. The A.I.A. was silent. Very well then, he would have to get along without their seal of approval. He had done just that for—what was it now?—35 years. Yes, so it was. Thirty-five years since the day of his arrival in Wells Street station with $7 in his pocket. With luck, he'd have another 35 years to go, he hoped. And damn the A.I.A. He didn't need them, and if they thought they didn't need him either? Well, they were wrong.

They might not need him, but architecture did, and America did. Some people were already beginning to know this, even if the A.I.A. didn't. Some people were beginning to catch on to the fact that there was a spirit, a *feeling* about a Frank Lloyd Wright building whether it was a house or a church or a hotel. People didn't only look at a Frank Lloyd Wright building, they experienced it. They didn't just shrug their shoulders at a Frank Lloyd Wright building, or pass it off with a polite expression of like or dislike. They expressed themselves with some passion. They loved or they hated the feeling it gave them. They loved or they hated the way it looked—which meant, what it stood for.

It stood for an idea that Wright considered the American idea. There was nothing bland or anonymous or conformist about any of Frank Lloyd Wright's buildings. There was nothing traditional about them except in the sense that respect for the individual human being and his need for shelter, for beauty, for closeness to nature, and for freedom from tyranny were deeply ingrained in the American spirit. So, in this American sense, Wright's buildings were traditional, in that they respected man's basic needs and tried to fulfill them. The youth and vigor and inventiveness of the American spirit were also reflected in Wright's architecture. So were the romantic longings of a young nation, still not too far removed from the days of the frontier.

[*127*]

Strangely enough, encouragement and comfort to this American architect continued to arrive mostly from abroad: a European, Kuno Francke, who had visited Wright in Oak Park and first persuaded him to go to Europe to meet his fellow architects there; a publisher in Berlin who brought out the first serious book about Wright's early work; an Emperor in Japan who entrusted him with his first substantial commission. Again Europe and the Far East recognized him now as the master builder that he was, and turned to him to learn.

Other letters on his desk comforted him for the absence of recognition from the A.I.A. From all over the world young people were writing to Frank Lloyd Wright, wanting to come to Taliesin, Wisconsin, U.S.A. Well, yes, thought Frank Lloyd Wright, let them come. Let them come to Taliesin, Wisconsin, U.S.A. It was time for America to play her part in the rising sun of architecture. It was time for give and take between the old world and the new, the past and the present—and the future that both worlds would share in. Wright and Taliesin both would go quietly to work again Americanizing Europe . . . or Europeanizing America? It was a learning process and so a changing and a growing one, either way.

Wright would be glad to see the fires lit once more at Taliesin, and the hill farm cultivated, and the discussions and the music resumed, and the work go ahead. He would be glad to see Taliesin come alive.

Come alive! Yes, that was it. That was always the trick.

"Come alive, boy!" Wright could hear Lieber Meister's words over his shoulder as though it were yesterday.

Wright turned slowly to the last unopened letter on his desk. The Master's hand had been shaking when he wrote it. The Master—Louis Sullivan—was dying.

Chapter 14

The End of an Era

The old Warner Hotel on Cottage Grove Avenue had nothing to recommend it but the fact that Louis Henri Sullivan chose to live out the last days of his life there. Shabby, down at the heels, as dilapidated as its neighborhood and as brave with its sad remnants of bygone finery, the Warner suited the old Master's mood. Sometimes Frank Lloyd Wright came to town and persuaded him to spend a night or two at the fashionable new Congress Hotel. Once Sullivan even agreed to motor back across the Illinois plains and up to Spring Green, Wisconsin, with Frank. But it was too late for the fresh country air and the smell of woods and earth to do the Master any good. A bad cold in the head was all he had to show for his visit to Taliesin.

So, in the end, Louis Sullivan waited for death in his own cluttered bedroom at the Warner, or on good days, put on his fine brown suit and took his stick and presented himself to the doorman of the Cliff Dwellers. The Cliff Dwellers, an architects' club, offered him the comfort of an armchair by the fireside, a writing table with plenty of paper, pens, and fresh ink, and the occasional visit of a friend. He had a lifetime membership in the Cliff Dwellers—the least his friends could do for him. Louis Sullivan was a proud man. He did not want charity. He wanted work. This was one thing, however, that no one could do for him. The world had passed him by.

After the Columbian Exposition he had prophesied that the turn to "classicism" would strike a death-blow to American architecture for half a century if not more. Well, it seemed he was right. Gone were the exciting days of the turn of the century, the dreams of a new society, of a new architecture, the days of Chicago's proud, free, ambitious spirit. War was over, peace secured, and the world made safe for democracy. But it was not Louis Sullivan's brand of democracy. It was something else.

"People don't think any more, Wright," he said one day. "You couldn't build those radical buildings we once built. They wouldn't let you. Mediocrity is today's catchword."

True or false, this was the way the world looked to Louis Sullivan in the 1920's. The chase for the almighty and elusive dollar was faster than ever. The old struggle of the individual to be himself, to treasure his uniqueness, to express his humanity didn't seem to count any more. Humanism was an old-fashioned 19th century notion. The world had begun to move too fast. It had no time for genius. Besides, how could you put a price tag on imagination, after all?

But Louis Sullivan was not to be bypassed so easily. Failing health did not stop him any more than the ignorance or indifference of the new brand of conformity to his genius had stopped him. Louis Sullivan still had something to say; and if no one would pay him to say it in stone or terra-cotta or steel, then he would say it in words. Day after day at his writing table in the Cliff Dwellers, he added page after page to his *Autobiography of an Idea*.

"Listen to this, Frank," he would say, and his brown eyes burning as brightly as ever, he would read aloud to his former apprentice until a coughing fit would overcome him, or shortness of breath force him to put the pages down. "Another day, Frank."

Another day, and another week, and another chapter. Wright took to coming to Chicago as often as he could. Sullivan's hand shook; his heart pounded; he needed to be helped across the street and up the curbstones. It couldn't last much longer. The strong black coffee he loved wasn't helping any; but it was too late to matter much, anyway, his doctor said.

"Listen to this, Frank . . ." and Frank listened, moved more than he cared to say by the fact that Lieber Meister finally called him gently by his first name instead of the old peremptory "Wright!" or even "Boy!"

Sullivan's *Autobiography* flowed and sparkled and came to life, as his drawings had. The New England landscape with its fields and streams and woods, the streets of Boston where he had been born, the dunes and the ocean at Cape Ann, the dusty discipline of the schoolrooms whose desks and textbooks he pored over, whose instructors he debated with—all came alive!

Then: Chicago! Louis Sullivan at 17 years old coming West to be an architect when Frank Lloyd Wright was just beginning to discover the magic of the kindergarten blocks his mother had brought him home from the St. Louis Fair.

Yes, the road that had led to Chicago for both of them had started half a century ago, when Louis Sullivan, son of an Irish father named Patrick and a French-Italian mother named Adrienne, born and bred in New England, boarded a train one evening in New York's Pennsylvania Station and headed West.

Morning came; the New Englander looked out of his

train window at the landscape flashing by.

"He was utterly amazed," read Sullivan from the flowing pages of his manuscript. "He was amazed and bewildered at his first sight of the prairies. How could such things be! The prairies—stretching like a floor to the far horizon. Here was power! And a great lake, spreading also like a floor to the far horizon, superbly beautiful in color, under a lucent sky. Here again was power. And over all spanned the dome of the sky. Here, in full view, was the light of the world, companion of the earth, a power greater than the lake and the prairie below, but not greater than man in his power: so Louis thought."

And so Louis wrote, and so Frank listened, his own memories and dreams, and his own visions of the things still to be accomplished reawakened by the courage of the master.

"The train neared the city," read Louis Sullivan, and Frank listening remembered too, "it broke into the city; it plowed its way through miles of shanties disheartening and dirty gray. It reached its terminal at an open shed. Louis tramped the platform, stopped, looked toward the city, ruins around him; looked at the sky; and as one alone, stamped his foot, riased his hand and cried in full voice:

THIS IS THE PLACE FOR ME!

That day was the day before Thanksgiving in the year Eighteen Hundred Seventy-three."

On April 14, 1924, Louis Henri Sullivan died. The day before he died, the first bound copy of the *Autobiography* had just come in. It was lying on the table beside his bed. He asked his friend Frank to help him up. Sitting on the edge of the bed, his friend's overcoat across his shoulders, his friend's arm around him to keep him warm and steady, he looked over at the book.

"Give me the book! The first copy to you. A pencil."

He tried to raise his arm to take the pencil; he couldn't lift it.

Frank Lloyd Wright left his friend's bedside at nightfall. Sullivan slept. Wright never saw him again. He had the "book"; he had a sheaf of drawings the Master had given him some weeks before; he had a family daguerrotype Sullivan had asked the nurse "to save for Frank," and he had a proud memory.

"What I am seeking," Frank had said to Lieber Meister only a few short weeks before, "is a genuine living architecture of the present." And he showed Sullivan the preliminary drawings for a skyscraper, a cantilevered glass office building, commissioned to house the National Life Insurance Company in Chicago. The building would be at least one-third lighter than any tall building yet built—and three times stronger. It would be balanced as a body on the legs, the walls hanging as the arms from the shoulder. Strong, light, steady, and able to be pre-fabricated in the shop, the National Life Insurance Building would be a shimmering fabric, a thing of delicate beauty, slender, iridescent by day, luminous by night.

"I dream of such a city," said Wright, "I know it can be built. A city that cleanses itself in the rain."

Sullivan studied the drawings.

"It is a work of art," he said. "I could never have done this building myself, but," he added with a smile, "I believe that, but for me, you could never have done it."

It was true. Frank Lloyd Wright acknowledged the debt,

acknowledged it proudly, and with gratitude.

"I know I should never have reached it," he wrote in his own autobiography, "but for what Sullivan was and what Sullivan himself did." He dedicated the National Life Insurance Building to Lieber Meister. It would be a living memorial, he thought, more fitting than the carved tombstone other fellow architects had commissioned to mark the grave of the 19th century genius, Louis Henri Sullivan, architect, teacher, friend.

"The free spirit is the spirit of joy," wrote Sullivan. "It delights to create in beauty. It is unafraid, it knows not fear. It declares the Earth to be its home, and the fragrance of the Earth to be its inspiration.

"Our dream shall be of a civilization founded upon ideas thrillingly sane, a civilization squarely resting on man's quality of virtue as a human being. Such dream is the vigorous daylight dream of man's abounding power, that he may establish in beauty and in joy, on the earth a dwelling place devoid of fear."

Chapter 15

On the Road

"A civilization thrillingly sane . . . a dwelling place devoid of fear . . ."

It did not happen quite that way; not in the 1920s'; not in Chicago; not in Spring Green, Wisconsin; not anywhere in the United States, not anywhere else in the world

Louis Sullivan died and nine years went by; and on March 4, 1933, a new President of the United States delivered his inaugural address to a nation with 13,000,000 unemployed.

In 1933, people were afraid. They had reason to be. They were experiencing the most savage depression the nation had ever known.

Frank Lloyd Wright's living memorial to Sullivan never got off the drawing board of 1925. Neither did his project for San Marcos in the Desert, an Arizona resort. Nor did his vision of an oilman's ranch in the California foothills, nor his plans for a Nevada recreation center on a lake, nor for a Wisconsin country club, for a cathedral to house all faiths, nor for a spiral planetarium climbing the crest of a Maryland mountain, nor for a glass and steel apartment tower, St. Marks in the Bowerie, to house New York city dwellers.

Nine years went by and the plans piled up—and so did the debts. Taliesin, once more destroyed by fire, was once more rebuilt, and once more deserted. The faithful core of apprentices and fellow architects who had made Taliesin live again for Frank Lloyd Wright melted away for lack of work, for lack of money. Weeds grew in the fields, and in the chapel yard across the valley, the graves of five Lloyd-Jones daughters and five Lloyd-Jones sons were now clustered around the slender marble obelisk gleaming white against the chapel evergreens. The death of Wright's mother, the redoubtable Anna,—at only 83 years old, her son said, seemed truly to mark the end of an era.

Mother gone, the Master gone, a beloved home as good as gone to the bankers and the mortgage holders, there was nothing much left for Frank Lloyd Wright to do but once more to take up the pencil, the T square, and the triangle. And once more take to the road.

He became for a while a journeyman-preacher. Although his pockets were empty, his fame had spread. People, young people particularly in universities and colleges across the country, wanted to know what he was all about. Many of the terms he used had begun to be part of an architectural vocabulary. A new language of architecture was in the making. New words began to be heard. What did they mean? Did they simply cloak old ideas? Or did they describe new ones?

New architects were beginning to be heard from, new "schools," and new "styles" talked about, in the United States in Sweden, in Germany, in Holland, in France, in Italy.

Was the sun of architecture really rising? and if so, what sort of shadow would its buildings cast upon the ground? Functional? Modern? Natural? Organic? International?

Frank Lloyd Wright decided he would answer a few questions. Or he would try to, at least.

".... as nearly organic as steel in tension and concrete in compression can make it. ...."

St. Mark's-in-the-Bouwerie, New York, perspective drawing

Museum of
Modern Art

Part Three:

As a Tree in the Midst of Nature

Chapter 16

"Child of the Spirit of Man"

B ecause the land is the simplest form of architecture, said Frank Lloyd Wright, the land is where the study of architecture begins.

In nature there is a continual process of "becoming," a process of growth and change, of birth and death, of decay and creation. The earth's landscape is a living landscape. The surface of the earth bears witness to its past, a past that was once long ago violent, that was alive in eras long gone by with the warring forces of wind and water, fire and ice, which fought for possession of this planet.

The same laws of change, of conflict, and of growth are still very much alive today. If we learn to look, said Frank Lloyd Wright, and to feel what goes on around us, we can discern the living history of this earth in the making. Day to day, hour by hour, minute after minute.

From their jagged heights against the sky, the slopes of the mountain ranges come, almost imperceptibly, ever more gently down to meet the plains; the teeming life of the forest floors ceaselessly prepares new seedlings to populate tomorrow's woods; the bluster of wind and the scouring of rain relentlessly alter the faces of the rocks and the profiles of the cliffs; hills and valleys form and re-form on the bottom of the sea, on the shifting desert sands. From the greatest of nature's manifestations to the smallest, from mountain peak to milk-weed pod, from the buffalo to the 17-year locust, there is continual movement, change; a continuous cycle of birth and death—and birth again.

There is also a basic unchanging principle at work, the law of nature reasserting order time and again over chaos. Nature is a tireless builder. She is inventive. She is imaginative. Nature invests her forms with infinite variety. She builds with cunning to preserve life. Hunt for the gray-green lichen, clinging almost unnoticed to the rock! Study the seashell's countless variations on a single theme: survival in a world of ceaseless movement!

Nature builds with economy to sustain life under many varying conditions of weather, temperature, and soil. Examine the cellular structure of a bamboo stalk! How slender and light it is; yet how strong, tough, and efficient! Look at the durable cactus, green and fleshy under a baking sun, its water-storing life-force guarded by thorns.

Nature builds with pattern and movement; the interplay of sun and shadow, of sound and stillness. Sun and a fresh breeze play with the dappled leaves of the young spring woods, the shadow of a cloud crosses a sunlit field; a grasshopper sings in the silence of noon.

Nature builds with color; like a candle-flame, the scarlet blossom of the Ocatilla flickers in the desert; cowslips dot a meadow; branches of coral drown in a turquoise sea.

Nature builds with design, breaks the long, horizontal earthline with a clump of trees, an outcropping of rock; leads the eye to a distant view of mountains or to the naked rim of the sky.

Everywhere there is pattern, rhythm, movement: on the

rippling surface of a pond, in the random passage of a butterfly over a field of flowers, in the myriad tracks of sandpiper, snail, sandcrab, and seagull on the shores and in the marshes.

Nature, always in the process of change, of "becoming," ceaselessly creates anew. Nothing Nature creates is arbitrary. Nothing is unrelated. Everything belongs. No part could exist without the whole. Without a leaf there would be no flower, without a stem no leaf, without its root no stem. Nature's forms have integrity. They have purpose, and they have beauty.

These three things—integrity, purpose, beauty—in Nature's hands are part of a permanent act of creation in a world of change.

Whenever man puts a building on this earth, he is also creating, said Frank Lloyd Wright. Architecture is a positive act of creation on man's part. Man's buildings say that he is in possession of his earth, that he is no less a part of the landscape than are the rocks or trees, the bears or bees who share the life-giving force of nature with him. To the extent that man remains close to the earth, true to the creative principles of nature—of order, integrity of purpose, of beauty, of repose—his buildings are architecture. True architecture is never "old," said Frank Lloyd Wright, nor will it ever be "new." True architecture is born out of the heart of man. It is the record of man in possession of his earth.

After the failure of early 20th century American architecture to live up to its promise, Frank Lloyd Wright began to look elsewhere. He began to look backwards, beyond the Renaissance of the 15th century, beyond the architecture of Rome and Greece, searching for an integrity he felt had been lost somewhere along the centuries. He found part of what he was looking for in the ancient civilizations, where there was still a closeness between people and the natural elements of the world they lived in. The great Mayan temples rose up out of the floors of the rain forests looking almost like masses of sculptured rock. The Egyptian monuments and pyramids rose up out of the red deserts and irrigated valleys of the Nile as though they too had been designed and erected by men who understood and took pride in the parched, vast, awesome land they lived so close to. Even the adobe pueblos of the American Southwest and the tepees of the nomadic Navajo performed their basic functions of providing shelter from sun and rain, the winter winds, and summer storms with dignity and naturalness, without artifice, with truth.

Architecture, said Frank Lloyd Wright, from its earliest beginnings down through the ages expressed man's way of making himself at home on this earth, of *being himself* in his environment. A building, if it wanted to be considered architecture and not simply a structure of one sort or another, ought to express man's spirit, his feeling about himself and the world he lived in. A man's home offered him comfort and shelter, yes. It ought also to inspire him with a sense of order, of harmony, of beauty, of kinship with the earth. For the search for harmony and beauty, for order and intelligence are an integral part of man's spirit, as organically a part of man's purpose as they are instinctively a part of Nature's.

This was what Wright meant when he said a building ought to grow out of human conditions, as a plant grows out of soil. A building ought to be free to be itself, to live its own life according to man's nature. Then, he said, you could truly call it architecture: a building "dignified as a tree in the midst of nature, but a child of the spirit of man."

[144]

The Space Within

But what did all this have to do with *modern* architecture? Where was the "new" vocabulary, where were the "new" terms, the "new" styles? What did *modern* really mean?

To understand what modern really meant, said Frank Lloyd Wright, it was necessary first of all to understand what it did not mean, what was *not* architecture, and what had not been architecture since the Renaissance when architecture had first lost its way. Architecture in the Renaissance had lost sight of the meaning of true form as an expression of purpose. It had confused form with style. When architecture began to think in terms of style instead of in terms of purpose, or function, it ceased to have integrity. Architecture was no longer creative, no longer born of the heart of man.

To explain further what had happened to architecture, Frank Lloyd Wright went back to his own early days, to the 1890's, when the Queen Anne style or the English Tudor style or the Neo-Classic style were what the pacesetters of American culture were ordering from their architects. America was a young country, he said, but it had not yet learned the power of its own youth, or to trust in its own convictions.

America borrowed culture, imitated past styles, frowned on the strength of its own artistic potentials. The architecture of the 1890's and the early 1900's turned its back on the changes the 20th century was bringing into the life of man. It did not take advantage of new inventions, new machines, new materials. It was no longer a record of *modern* man in possession of his earth. Modern man was wearing hand-me-downs in his houses. He was wearing architectural "styles" that fitted him no better than a suit of armor.

Instead of helping modern man to achieve a new sense of freedom and dignity in his houses, the new materials, inventions, and machines had been put to work to reconstruct something out of somebody else's past. Or they had been put to work by the self-styled "modernists" to build him a soulless house, a house that looked itself like a machine.

Frank Lloyd Wright was the first to say that a house ought to be built by means of the machine. He was also the first to say that a house ought to be considered a kind of machine—a machine to live in. But this did not mean that a house should look like a machine. Machines were the means to an end, not the end itself. A square concrete box, or an aluminum cookie-tin was not much of an improvement over a pseudo-Spanish castle as a dwelling place for modern man.

So much for "styles," said Frank Lloyd Wright. Forget styles. Remember the lessons of Nature. Nature is a better teacher by far. Yes, a *modern* teacher. As nature puts her materials to work for her with integrity, purpose, and imagination, so must man. Nature does not strive for effects. Why should man? Man's architecture should be as *organic* as nature's. And here was the first new word Frank Lloyd Wright contributed to the language of modern architecture.

Architecture to be modern must be organic, said Frank Lloyd Wright. Organic did not mean a new style or a new

[146]

look. It meant an attitude, and so it was hard to define and it was often misused; it still is.

If a man really thought directly about any problem in architecture, Lieber Meister had once said, the solution would emerge from the character of the problem itself. He didn't impose a solution. He didn't arbitrarily decide upon a style. He studied the problem and let his imagination go to work. This, of course, was Nature's own way of solving her problems. And it became Frank Lloyd Wright's way, the way he called *organic*.

If he was going to build a house on a hill, he did not level off the top of the hill to make it fit the house. He did quite the opposite. The house he built on a hillside did not ignore or deny its site; it dramatized it. He studied the hill, the lines of the slope, the silhouette against the sky, the nature of the soil, the way the vegetation grew, the passage of the sun, and the direction of the winds. He built a house that seemed to grow out of the hillside in a natural way. This was one of the things Frank Lloyd Wright meant by the word organic. He did not imitate Nature, but he understood and made use of the same principles Nature used.

Again, as in Nature the flower is organically related to the leaf and the leaf to the stem and the stem to the root, so in architecture the word organic also meant that the separate members of a house—the rooms, the stairs, the windows, the ceilings, the walls—should be related to each other in a similar way. Organic meant, then, that the part should be related to the whole, and that the whole—the house and its landscape—should be a living, functioning thing. It should serve its purpose with integrity and beauty.

If this was the aim, then of course the architect had to

[*147*]

start thinking about a house in an entirely different way. He thought first of all of its purpose. Its purpose was humane.

He was not building monuments of the past or museums for posterity. He was building a living architecture for a living people, said Frank Lloyd Wright, and he began to call his architecture the architecture of democracy—the architecture of the free individual in a democratic society. The principle of growth and of change was a democratic principle as surely as it was a natural principle. In a democratic society a man had freedom, and he had conscience. He did not need to be "boxed-in" either by his form of government—or by the four walls of his house.

If all these thoughts were in the back of an architect's mind—how a man ought to be able to live in a house with comfort and a sense of adventure and freedom—then he stopped thinking about the four walls first. He stopped thinking about a house from the top down and the outside in. He began thinking about a house from the ground up—and from the inside out.

Frank Lloyd Wright had begun to think this way back in the 1890's. The Prairie Houses were the first results of Wright's thinking in terms of an organic house. There, in the center of the Prairie House, in "the heart" of the house as Wright liked to say, was the great fireplace, and from it the house moved out in long, low lines of serenity and repose, following the long low horizontal earth-lines of the prairie itself. The man who lived in the Prairie House felt sheltered under its protective eaves, comforted at its fireside, and he felt himself at the same time drawn by the very horizontal lines of the house itself towards the out-of-doors. His windows were not bars to nature; they were an invitation to the natural world. His walls did not close him in; they merely screened him from the wind and the rain.

One thought led to another as they usually do, and Frank Lloyd Wright began to find himself thinking more and more not primarily of how a house would look, but of how it would *feel*. Up popped once more the "new" idea which—he had discovered in Japan—wasn't so new, after all, an idea born 2,300 years before Frank Lloyd Wright. This idea that Frank Lloyd Wright rediscovered, first given voice to by Lao-tsu, an idea that had become a working reality in the wood and paper houses of Japan, Wright called "the space within."

In its simplest terms, the "space within" had to do with how the rooms were laid out on a floorplan. The feeling of spaciousness entered into it, of course. Abandoning the notion of rooms as a series of boxes within a box, he came up with something that architects began to call the "open floor plan"—and have been using in one form or another ever since.

But there was more than that to the idea of the "space within." There was something to the idea of "space" itself. Space was something to be used, Wright discovered, just as tangibly, as realistically and as creatively as any of the other elements in architecture.

Space was not simply an abstract idea. It was something to work with—yes, to use as color, light and shadow, texture of materials, mass, site and the rest of the elements that together created the substance and feeling of a house were used. The way an architect used the element of space in designing a house affected more than any other single factor the way people felt in that house. They could feel cramped or uplifted, comforted or inspired, crowded or serene, sheltered or vulnerable, restless or relaxed, depending. . .

From the 1930's on, Frank Lloyd Wright began to use the element of space in architecture in a new way. He began to consider walls and ceilings, corridors and stairs, doorways and archways and windows not only as the usual means of limiting space, but as a means of defining space, shaping space, even dramatizing it. The Prairie Houses had already begun to dramatize man's feelings about himself in relation to the earth. Now the houses of the '30's began to dramatize man's feelings about himself in space, in inner space, that is—not in the stratosphere or the ionosphere or the atmosphere around Mars. But here on earth.

A child does not have to be taught what space is. He finds out for himself, even though he may forget it later on. Long before he can put his thoughts or feelings into words, he plays with space. He experiments with it. He also dramatizes it. Sometimes, for instance, he likes to find out how big space is—and how small he is. Sometimes it is the other way around. Sometimes he hides in closets. Sometimes he roars around the living room and races up and down the stairs. He feels small and alone on the great bare stage of the school auditorium. He feels safe and protected in the corner of the living room couch by the fireside. He scares himself and he reassures himself, exposes himself and shelters himself, depending on his mood.

Sometimes he likes to bring everything down to his size, to cram the whole world into the tiny "space" below the kitchen table where he plays for hours. Sometimes he likes to conquer the universe, swooping up and down and cross it in a high-flying swing, or building a tree house in the topmost branches to look down in disdain on the little people below.

[*150*]

In all these ways and many more he is experimenting with himself in space, and in light and shadow, and in relation to the earth and sometimes to the sky.

The new building materials and methods of the 20th century freed architecture from the limitations of the old four-square, post-and-beam construction of the box. Wright had already discovered what that freedom could mean: in the use of the cantilever, for instance, in the Imperial Hotel: in the use of reinforced concrete; in the use of glass and the liberation of the window to be, making it not merely a hole in the wall but an invisible curtain, a screen, a canvas on which the architect could paint with Nature's own light and shadow, color and texture.

All these developments in building materials and principles of construction meant that it was now possible for the architect to create interior space with imagination, and to experiment with various forms, more flexible forms than had ever been used before, forms for living.

Nor was it necessary for the organic architect to sacrifice beauty—or romance, as Wright called it—to functionalism. Poetry was the sound of the heart, said Wright, and if a house had no poetry—or joy—or beauty—it had no heart. It had lost its humane purpose. It had ceased to be something for a human being to live in.

With imagination and a new freedom, the cube, the triangle, and the sphere that Wright had got to know as a small boy so intimately on his kindergarten table from the Froebel Gifts now began to take on new significance in the architect's shaping of the "space within."

"We've got to break America out of the box!" Frank Lloyd Wright had cried out to Cecil on a long-ago summer

[151]

evening in the midst of a dusty suburban Chicago street. "I'll find the way. I've got to."

Well, he did. He found many ways. He built houses that were hexagonal, triangular, rectangular, circular, hemispheric, that were spiral. He built houses that surmounted a cliff, spanned and straddled a waterfall, hung out over a lake, swirled up out of a desert, sloped down to a gentle meadow. He built houses that he called "Wingspread" and "Snowflake," "Suntop" and "Fountainhead," "Deertrack" and "Ocatilla," and he built "Fallingwater."

None of these forms into which Frank Lloyd Wright shaped the "space within" was arbitrarily decided upon. He let the contours of the land guide him—and the needs of his clients: the way they lived, the view they loved to look at, the privacy they wanted, the family living they did together; the books, art, music; the games of children; the ritual of the dinner table. It all belonged, the indoors and the outdoors, the ways of nature and the needs of man; it all belonged to the new freedom he called organic architecture.

Before he was through—and in 1930 he was far from through!—he built more than 300 buildings in 34 of the United States. No two were alike. None followed a set pattern. Each had its own feeling and served its own purpose and fit its own site. And—some were more successful than others! Like every other architect, Frank Lloyd Wright was guilty of a roof that leaked and a fireplace that didn't draw and a floor that refused to be properly warmed by the heating unit under it, and green lumber that warped, and draughts that came sneaking around corners where they weren't supposed to, and budgets that mysteriously skyrocketed, and clients who didn't like what they thought they wanted when they got it!

[152]

Some people called him a bully and a tyrant. Some people called him the kindest man who ever lived. Some people called him a clown. No doubt at one time or another in his life he was one or another of these things or sometimes all of them at once.

The interesting things was that, different as his houses were one from the other, yet they had something in common, all of them. People wanted to know what this something was. Students wanted to know if they could learn to do it too. Granted that each building was an individual act of creation on the architect's part, wasn't there some sort of formula you could follow?

Over and over again, the architect was questioned. What exactly did he mean by this? and what exactly did he mean by that?

And over and over again, the journeyman-preacher gave his answers. Yes, for the rest of Wright's life, the questions went on being asked, and the answers kept on being given. What Wright said always boiled down to more or less the same sort of thing, the same basic ideas, the same "principles" expressed in one way or another.

"A house . . . ." said Wright. . . "should be natural. Anything organic is natural and almost always anything natural is organic."

*". . . with the comfort of a wide, low roof
to anchor it where it belongs."*

The Robie House, Chicago, Illinois, 1909

"True ornament is the inherent melody of structure."

Detail of the exterior of La Miniatura, 1923

Ezra Stoller Associates

*. . . by way of steel in tension this building takes its place
and achieves its form."*

Detail of exterior of Fallingwater, Bear Run, Pennsylvania, 1936

Bill Hedrich, Hedrich-Blessing

"He loved the site . . . and liked to listen to the waterfall . . . a prime motive in the design. . . ."

Fallingwater

Bill Hedrich, Hedrich-Blessing

Fallingwater

*"The cantilever is most romantic, most free
of all principles of construction."*

Part Four:

The Phoenix and the Desert

Chapter 18

Organic Architecture

In the spring of 1939, in London, Frank Lloyd Wright, the newest honorary member of the Royal Institute of British Architects reiterated, "What a man does, that he has." Then he went on, "We're going to carve those words in oak over the entrance to our drafting room. They stand for something we believe in. They sum up the new adventures we're headed for. They stand for an idea, the idea of organic architecture as a working reality. And when this idea begins to take hold, to take root, to go to work in the mind of the young architect, something happens. Something happens to life. We—all of us—begin once more to want to live like spirited human beings. . . ."

Something spirited was certainly happening to the life of the audience who had come to hear this year's Sir George Watson Chair lecturer. The Sir George Watson Chair went, by annual invitation, on alternate years to a Britisher and an American. The invitation carried much prestige with it and a $2,500 honorarium. The lecturer could make one speech— or ten; the number didn't matter. What did matter was that what he said should add something of value to the growing cultural understanding between Britain and America.

Lecturers over the years past had included an august procession of politicians and statesmen, presidents and governors, academicians and jurists. The present holder of the chair, of course, was none of these. He held, as a matter of fact, no office, had no regular degrees of any kind. Without any question at all, however, he did hold his audience.

It was the second of an announced four lectures on the uncompromising topic, "An Organic Architecture." The hall was, if possible, even more crowded than it had been the week before. The seats had filled. Standing room was gone. It finally became clear that latecomers would have to be turned away at the door. The moderator for the evening, the distinguished Earl of Crawford, leaned across the platform and said to the lecturer in well-bred tones of astonishment, "What is this, Mr. Wright? The Board has never seen anything like this before."

"Your lordship," said Frank Lloyd Wright with a twinkle in his eyes, "I can't imagine."

It was mainly a young audience, made up mostly of university students, and it was by no means a docile one. It was an audience prepared politely and firmly—in the best British tradition of the best British audiences—to heckle. And heckle it did, with intelligence and with spirit. The audience delighted the lecturer. So did the hecklers, not all of whom stood up bravely on the floor. Some of then—including a dowager duchess barricaded behind her lorgnette and an elderly peer of the realm chomping on his moustaches—contented themselves with *sotto voce* comments about this "upstart" iconoclast from over the sea.

An iconoclast Frank Lloyd Wright certainly was. One could hardly say that age had mellowed him. If anything, age had sharpened his wit, his appetite for controversy, and his hunger for new experience. He was almost 70 on that spring evening in London, 1939. Yet he disappointed no one by the tameness of his views. None of the old fire was gone. He was as uncompromising as ever. And he was by no means ready to retire from the architectural scene, even though his 50 years of practice had brought him almost as much frustration and disappointment as it had brought him fame. "Add tired to tired" was what Frank Lloyd Wright had been doing all his life. He was still doing it, and he was still loving it.

He looked down at his audience and for a clear, flashing moment, he thought to himself: "What am I doing here? I'm not a talker, I'm a builder. A doer. Go on home and get it done, Frank! Build it! Do it!" The moment passed, and Frank Lloyd Wright went right on talking, expounding his views, trying to communicate something of his own excitement, his own sense of wonder, to those who had come to hear him. But before this moment had altogether passed, Frank Lloyd Wright took his audience into his confidence. Anyone who wanted to, or was able to, could read between the lines of what he said.

"I could be, as I stand here," he said, "a bitterly disappointed old man. I am not. I am quite happy and still interested in the thing I love. You have no lecturer before you tonight, but an emissary of the ground, preaching the salt and savor of a new and fresh life. You might say of me," he added, looking down at his own hands as if to reassure himself that these fingers would soon again be holding a pencil and driving it in swift, clean strokes across the sheet of white paper, "you might say of me that I am simply a worker—in from the field."

The "field" the worker was in from, was of course the

beloved Valley of Wright's boyhood, of the Lloyd-Jones uncles and aunts, of the chapel in the woods and—of *Truth Against the World*.

The paths a man found himself following in pursuit of Truth Against the World were many and varied. Nor were they to be followed without pain, disappointment, and grief, Frank Lloyd Wright had discovered. It was not always easy to keep the flag of courage flying bravely in the face of frustration. Then, too, he had discovered courage was not always enough to sustain a man. Not courage alone. Something else was needed. Something—or someone—else.

Like many another man in pursuit of an ideal, Frank Lloyd Wright had had his setbacks. Like many another artist, he had felt at times unwanted, misunderstood, deprived of his rightful place in the world, deprived, that is, of the chance to give freely and creatively the way he knew he was meant to. But he was not a man to turn his back on life. He went more than halfway to meet it. No matter how many times he was turned down, he always ended up by pounding on the door again and demanding to be let in. He was not one to nurse his wounds for long in silent self-pity, or to satisfy himself merely by making angry noises against whoever or whatever it was that had hurt him. Oh yes, he made the angry noises all right. He had become famous for the angry noises he made—usually with a twinkle in his eye—against the so-called civilization of cities; against the hidebound rigidities of school education; against the abuse of a man's talents resulting from his pursuit of the dollar instead of the good of mankind. All his life he had made angry noises against whatever he considered sham, or humbug, or hypocrisy. And all his life he spoke out and he acted on behalf of freedom.

It took him a good many years to find out that what he meant by freedom in a personal sense, at least, was something that happened inside a man. He meant inner freedom, he discovered. And how did a man get that?

You could break out of the architectural box of pseudo-styles and false traditions into architectural freedom; you could break out of the political box of authoritarianism into the political freedom of the individual in a democratic society; but breaking out of the personal box into a personal freedom was something else again. Perhaps, Wright began to think, the sense of personal freedom came another way. Perhaps personal freedom came not so much as a result of what you broke out of as what you built up within you. This didn't happen overnight. Nor, if you were restless and sometimes impatient and often stubborn, did it happen without heartbreak, without mistakes.

Looking back on the half-century that lay behind him, Frank Lloyd Wright had to acknowledge the price that he—and sometimes others—had paid for his right to pursue "truth" and freedom." Had it cost him too dearly? Could he have done otherwise? What had he learned after all?

He could not answer the first question. It was unanswerable. The second question he could and did answer. No, he could not have done otherwise. He had *had* to break out of the boxes that threatened to immure him, the barriers that would not let him move forward. He had to move forward. He had had to break out of boyhood, out of the university life which could no longer contain his creative urges; he had had to break away from apprenticeship—even from his beloved Lieber Meister, he had to be on his own as an artist; and he had had to break away from the Oak Park Studio when his heart was no longer in it—he had to move forward, even at the cost of leaving behind him a marriage that in its early years had promised, and had given, so much. All this in the name of truth and of freedom. How much of truth and freedom had he found?

As an artist, yes, he had forged ahead, so far ahead that it took 50 years or more before others began to catch up with him, before some of his ideas, at least began to catch on. And he was still out in front. At 80, he was to be called by many the greatest living architect. He was never a back number, not Frank Lloyd Wright!

But as a man, how had he fared in the "new life" he had entered into so bravely with the building of Taliesin I in the Valley of his forefathers? Taliesin I brought dramatically to the ground by fire a few short years later taught Wright the twin lessons of loneliness and despair. To be alone, he discovered, was not necessarily to be free. The artist, or the man, or both, needed someone to share life with, to share dreams—and disappointments, too.

Unhappily, Frank Lloyd Wright's second wife, as it soon turned out, either could not or would not share either. And once again the son of the Welsh pioneers and the Yankee preacher found himself, at 60, alone and an outcast. Once again society frowned, growled, gossiped; called him unregenerate, a rebel, eccentric, lawless. He didn't bother to deny any of it. Nor did he bother to deny to himself, at any rate, that he was lonelier than ever.

No, this did not seem to be the path to inner freedom. Taliesin II, in spite of the Valley's tender boyhood memories, in spite of the magical presence of the druid gods, in spite of the handful of faithful apprentices, in spite of the host of

visiting celebrities—artists, musicians, writers, statesmen—
of neighbors from across the way, in spite of all this, Taliesin
II was a lonesome place.

The weeds that choked the fields and hillsides were
sown not only by the depression years of debts and mort-
gages. They were the weeds sown by neglect, neglect of a man
as well as of an artist. The artist even during these lonesome
years, grew in stature and in fame. The name and face and
figure and the ideas of Frank Lloyd Wright began to become
familiar to thousands across the country. The man? well, he
was still in pursuit of truth and of freedom, and of something
he began to call faith.

Taliesin III was built, incredibly, on the ashes of Taliesin II, after fire had once more raged through the rooms of
the house of the North and destroyed many of the treasures
the builder had brought back from the Morning Land of
Japan.

Taliesin III rose from the ashes like the fabled phoenix
to celebrate not only freedom, truth, and courage, but to celebrate faith in life. A life that was now, finally, to be shared
with understanding and vision. A life that was to permit and
inspire the growth of the inner freedom Wright had sought
so long in vain.

On a midsummer day in August, Frank Lloyd Wright
and Olga Iovanovna Milanoff were married. Taliesin began
once more to hum with life—and with work. There were
crops in the fields; blueprints blossomed on the drawing
boards; new buildings took shape on the hills. Taliesin began
to build again—to build architects!

"Young architects," Frank Lloyd Wright told his London audience in 1939, "should not be seated in lecture-halls, even like this one. Or seated in classrooms, for that matter. They should be out on the ground somewhere. They should be working."

An empty statement? Well, hardly! To back it up, he had brought films with him to show what he meant, to show how the young apprentices-in-residence at Taliesin worked and lived the life he was talking about; and learned, of course, as they went about their daily tasks.

"I do not want you to have the idea that Taliesin is a school, or a community. It happens to be our home and where we work, and these young people are my comrade apprentices; no scholars. There are very many things to do because we have several hundred acres of 'farm,' and we are practicing architects in addition. So," said Wright, with an air of modesty that fooled no one, as the lights went out and the film unrolled, "as you can see, we are fairly busy."

Busy they were! those 23 apprentices-in-residence and Mr. and Mrs. Wright, and the half-dozen or so "senior" apprentices who had graduated to be full-time architects, supervising one or another of the commissions that had finally begun to come into Taliesin when the lean years of the depression were over.

No, it was not a school. It was difficult to describe exactly what the Taliesin Fellowship, as it was called, actually was. The Fellowship was most definitely not a school, said Wright, nor was he a teacher. All the same, of the thousand or more young men and women who came into the Fellowship during the years of its existence, a good number emerged as full-fledged professionals—architects, artists, writers, and builders. Who taught them? What and how did they learn?

[*168*]

Mr. Wright taught them, of course, deny it as he might. He taught them the way he himself had learned. He taught them to *see* and he taught them to *do*. He taught them to *work*. And he taught them, by example, as any good teacher does, to *think*.

"So we begin this working Fellowship as a kind of a daily work-life" announced the first circular of the Taliesin Fellowship in the summer of 1932. And by fall, the first 23 young men and women had arrived at Taliesin, ready to go, eager to leave off what Frank Lloyd Wright called "rocking in an old academic boat," eager to come to terms with the kind of freedom and responsibility Taliesin offered.

Needless to say, it was not all smooth sailing. "No more drawing-board architects at Taliesin, if I can help it," said Wright, and he meant it. He led youth into action by way of the axe, the saw, the plane, the hammer and the scythe, the shovel and the hoe. Learning to wield the stone chisel and the paint brush, neither more nor less than learning to get a meal on the table, flowers arranged in a vase, or costumes ready for a fancy dress festival, led ultimately to T-square and triangle on the drawing board.

All this was second-nature, of course, to Frank Lloyd Wright who dawn after summer dawn so long ago had awakened in an attic bedroom in these very hills to the banging on the stovepipe and the sound of his uncle's voice calling him to work; who had brought the cows in from the fields, chopped wood, pitched hay, and harvested crops till his arms ached; who had drowsed over the heaped-up table at dinner time, listening to the stories and the men's talk until his eyelids simply closed and his head went down to meet his folded arms. Now the gospel of work as the Lloyd-Joneses had preached and lived it came to life again for a new generation of young Americans, many of them ill prepared to meet anything but textbooks, or to create anything but term papers. Some of them stuck it out and learned, discovering for themselves the joy that took the drudgery out of work and made it creative. Some went away, claiming that hoeing a row of beans or helping an 80-year-old stonemason lay a wall had little or nothing to do with the practice of architecture.

The daily work-life of those first few years was more than the restating of a pioneer gospel. It was a matter of necessity if the Fellowship was to continue. Twenty-three young people had to be housed; drafting rooms had to be built; food had to be rounded up; and cash was the one commodity no one had very much of! Necessity, as usual, proved the mother of invention.

Lumber? Yes, lumber, the first requisite for any building program at Taliesin was available—for cash! Pay right now—or else! The Fellowship chose "or else"! They went into the logging business. After the logging business was attended to and Taliesin itself looked more like a loggers' camp than a community of architects and their apprentices, Taliesin went into the lumbering business. Seventy-thousand home sawn board feet of lumber was the result—to say nothing of the number of aching muscles, blisters, calluses, sunburned backs, and enormous appetites that also resulted. Never mind, the buildings were on their way up—and the "drawing-board architects" were on their way out.

"You've got to get the feel of the rock in your hands, m' boys," said old Charlie Curtis the weatherbeaten Cornish mason. So the apprentices went to work in the old stone quarries. Soon pile upon pile of the buff colored sandstone blocks stood about the skeletons of the buildings. Soon long, fine, stone walls began to take shape.

Yes, lime was available, too. Lime was the next requisite for the building program at Taliesin. Lime was available on the same terms as lumber. Cash, no credit. Pay up—or else! Again, the Fellowship chose "or else!" and they went into the lime business.

Up over the hills behind the old Hillside School buildings went Frank Lloyd Wright in his "prideful" Cord automobile. If the Cord had seen better days—and it had!—no one dared mention the fact out loud. The Cord had been intended —no more than had its predecessors the Packard, the Cadillac, the Stoddard-Dayton, the old Knox, the Overland Country Club, to be a beast of burden. The Cord was a thing of beauty; and prideful indeed, the Cord assumed its new duties with no loss of dignity. If the Master could haul groceries with no loss of dignity, or go roaring off along backcountry roads, up and over the crests of the hills to rout out an old kiln remembered from 25 years ago, well, the Cord would have to keep its end up. And it did!

Wright and the Cord found their way into the hill place of farmer August Cupps, tall, awkward, a maker of sorghum molasses.

"Sure," said August, "the old kiln's still around. Needs fixing up, though."

"We'll fix her up," said Wright.

"Needs wood to fire her," said August.

"Plenty of wood on the hill here," said Wright, pointing with his stick.

"So there is," said August. "Supposing I were to sell it to you for three-fifty a cord? Cut it myself. Plenty of limestone

[171]

—You want to dig it out?" They did.

The bargain was struck and Wright and the Cord set off in another direction, headed now for the backcountry town of Black Earth. Yes, there was still an old-time lime-burner around. Sure, he'd instruct the boys. Why not? It never hurt an old-timer to keep his hand in, did it? Soon the fires were roaring, and the old kiln on the hillside in the woods behind August's farm was burning day and night. The boys took turns sleeping on the ground beside her, getting up every two hours all night long to see she didn't go out.

You could see that light in the sky for miles around, night after night. You could see it from Taliesin. It was a good sight. It was good lime, too, and the burning of it in that old limekiln, the feeding of the fires all night long—the boys looking like stokers in the hold of a battleship, somehow seemed to sum up a little of what Frank Lloyd Wright meant when he talked about organic architecture as an adventure into reality, when he talked about living like a spirited human being.

Burning your own lime, logging and cutting your own lumber, growing your own food—no one ever sat down and figured out ahead of time that this was the way you built architects. There was no announcement of a curriculum that included lime burning or flower arranging, for that matter. What it amounted to was, very simply, that when you ran across a problem, you looked for the solution to it in the nature of the problem itself. You weren't afraid to think your way into or out of it. You weren't afraid to think in simples, as Wright said. When you saw what had to be done, you did it.

As a matter of fact, the whole *idea* of Taliesin Fellowship came to Wright as a result of just this kind of approach

[*172*]

to a problem. No buildings to build at that moment. A long moment, a moment that lasted seven years! Then why not build the builders of buildings? That was precisely what the Fellowship set out to do. Frank Lloyd Wright set out to build the builders of buildings—against that time when buildings would be built again. And when buildings did begin to be built again, Frank Lloyd Wright and the Fellowship were ready.

On July 20, 1936, the client millionaire Hibbard ("the Hib") Johnson of Racine, Wisconsin, contracted for the building: Johnson Wax. Two years later, after countless headaches, troubles with unions, buildings codes, the bureaucracy of building commissions; after the budget had been more than tripled; after 132 round trips had been made (in the prideful Cord) between Taliesin and Racine, the Johnson Wax building was finished. It caused, to put it mildly, quite an uproar. Thirty thousand people streamed through it in the first two days. Its fluent curves, graceful "lily-pad" columns; its airiness, lightness, and the creative simplicity of its design, all these convinced even the most hardened skeptic that the well of Frank Lloyd Wright's originality had by no means yet run dry. The last great period of his exploration into new forms, new uses of materials and new subleties of interior space had only just begun.

"Herbert Johnson said, 'Why not go up in the air, Frank?'
So we went up in the air."

S. C. Johnson & Son, Research Tower,
Racine, Wisconsin, 1950

Ezra Stoller Associates

"The new reality of the building is the interior space. This reality is modern."

Interior of S. C. Johnson & Son, Administration Building, Racine, Wisconsin, 1939

Chapter 19

The Journey Ends

Taliesin West—a look over the rim of the world!

The long journey which had started for Frank Lloyd Wright in an unassuming frame house in Richland Center, Wisconsin, in a room hung with framed prints of cathedrals of England, in a town set about with green fields and an indolent brown river, was to come to an end almost a century later in the sharp, clean, savage landscape of an Arizona desert.

"Going where I list, my own master. . . . Divesting myself of the holds that would hold me. I inhale great draughts of space. The east and the west are mine; the north and the south are mine. . . . " Yes, Walt Whitman wrote the words to this American dream, as Jefferson before him had voiced the philosophy of an American democracy. Frank Lloyd Wright loved the words, and lived them, pursued both dream and philosophy as nearly as any American ever had. Or possibly, to be more accurate about it, he lived them as nearly as any man ever could live them in a 20th century society whose complexities, whose powers for good and for evil, whose advances and retreats in the name of political progress, whose weapons against death—or towards it—whose scientific and technological achievements would have seemed unimaginable to a 19th century American.

Even though Frank Lloyd Wright's architecture was

[*177*]

very much of the 20th century, and in some of its concepts even beyond what contemporary architects have achieved today, yet Frank Lloyd Wright was a 19th century American and in many ways he remained one all his life. The frontiers of his boyhood may have vanished. But the pioneer spirit in Wright had not vanished; nor had the need for mobility, the restless urge to keep on the move; nor had the love for the soil, the desire to get back to the earth, to Nature's realities, to the "field."

In the Arizona desert Wright built a summer home for himself, his family, and the Fellowship. He called it Taliesin West. Others called it a fortress, a palace, a ship in full sail, the seat of empire of an Indian chieftain. As usual, everyone had something to say about it—for or against.

This is what another—a young—American architect had to say about Taliesin West and about Frank Lloyd Wright:

"Frank Lloyd Wright belongs to the ages. The essence of Taliesin West is the human element, the procession through the building. I once counted the turns that you make when you approach the building till you get into what he calls the Cove. And the number of turns, I think, was 45. Now, he is playing with you as you walk through that space. He stops your car, as any good architect should, two or three hundred feet from the entrance and then you start down steps, up steps; to the left, to the right; down the long, very long, pergola; and you turn to the right to get out onto that famous prow, and you take those few steps down onto the magnificent view that has been concealed from you for two or three hundred feet of walking, then you see Arizona stretched out, as he meant it to be.

"Then you turn and you go into the little tent room—

the man, of course, understands light better than anyone in the world—and he has this tent light that trickles, that filters down through into this private room. Before he opens any flaps, you're just bathed in this canvas light. Then when he opens the flap onto the little secret garden, you say there are no more surprises, there can't be any more unfolding of spaces —but there are! And, you get into this private courtyard with the green grass and the falling water and then you finally get into the Cove. Just when you're used to Frank Lloyd Wright's 6-foot ceiling, it has a 14-foot ceiling! And the fireplace runs the full length of the building! There are no windows all of a sudden, and no canvas! You are entirely enclosed in the middle of this—experience! And by the time you get there, you realize that you've been handled and twisted much as you are by a symphony until you get to the crisis."

Clearly, it was no easier than it ever had been to pin Frank Lloyd Wright's work down with a definition. Or to pin Wright down with a definition. Partly, this was because Wright *believed* in change. He distrusted rigidity. He thought it was never too late to learn.

"When you're learning," he said one Sunday morning to the members of his Fellowship assembled after breakfast in the great Taliesin living room for talk and the exchange of ideas, "when you're in the process of learning," Wright repeated, "you're in a state of becoming. That is what learning is. And the state of becoming is always. . . . a state of change."

"Try not to create a containment," he was heard to say to a young apprentice, and he leaned over the drawing board with pencil in hand to show what he meant. "Try to allow everything to come together in a fluid sense."

[*179*]

Waving his stick over his head, his mane of white hair nodding as he spoke, he explained himself this way to the reporter for an English journal, as they left the big drawing board in the drafting room of Taliesin West and walked out into the blazing Arizona sun: "Look for the central idea— then look for a form closely related to it that will express the idea. It takes some searching."

The stick touched plants and rocks and drew images in the sand and wandered around the outlines of a giant cactus. "Don't *start* to search at the drawing board. Think about it when you are out in a boat running ahead of a strong wind. Or walking through the fields. Don't start trying to draw until you can see the building in your mind. See it standing on the landscape. See the inside. Walk through the space inside in your mind—and when you have really seen it—draw like HELL."

"Also," added Frank Lloyd Wright, with the familiar twinkle in his eye, "it takes a genius to accomplish this!"

The word genius has been applied to Frank Lloyd Wright by others than himself. Less complimentary words have also been applied to him. The debate still rages today as it did when the Winslow House burst into flower on the Chicago prairie 50 years ago, and poor Mr. Winslow had to take the back road to the station to avoid the derision of his neighbors. No one argues any longer about one thing, however, and that is the value of the contributions Wright has made to the architecture of our time.

What are these contributions? Well, some of them are so familiar by now, it is hard to believe they have not always existed. It is hard to believe that they first took shape in the mind of one man who was willing half a century ago to look progress in the eye, to face the facts of the machine age, and to make creative use of new technological resources.

Here are a few of the many Frank Lloyd Wright "firsts": indirect lighting; the living room; the glass "wall" to let the outdoors in and the indoors out; the wall-hung toilet; the use of poured concrete non-industrially, of steel in tension, and the cantilever; radiant heating; the concept of the "space within."

Perhaps his greatest contribution to the architecture of our time was that he reinstated the architect as a responsible creator—not as an imitator of past styles, not as an errand boy, not as a file clerk of blue prints, but as an artist and a master builder. For this, the conventional, conformist architects of his own time hated him—"but for this, a new generation of architects, whose very profession he saved—honor him".

The artist in Frank Lloyd Wright, sometimes dormant but never extinct, came astonishingly to life in the last ten years of his life. For no artist is without his dry spells, and Frank Lloyd Wright was not an exception to the rule. The drought of the depression years came to an end with the building of Fallingwater, the imaginative, bold and romantic house in the Pennsylvania woods, cantilevered out over a waterfall. And with the Johnson Wax building, a whole new era began, in which, with a freedom even Wright himself had never shown before, he continued his explorations into interior space, and stated in more positive architectural terms than ever his belief that form and function were one.

The Racine Wax Tower: "It is a trunk with a taproot", Wright said, "carrying its floors like branches."

The Unitarian Church: "a triangle," said Wright, "the mass of its structure is depended upon to give the impression of aspiration usually left to a steeple."

[181]

The Price Tower: "Here again is the poise, balance, lightness, and strength that may characterize the creations of this age. . . . Now the skyscraper will come into its own on the rolling plains of Oklahoma."

Then, at last, into its own came the spiral. The seashell, perhaps the most intricate and cunning, the most varied and humble, perhaps the most beautiful of all of Nature's forms, is also, perhaps the most sophisticated. The mystery within the seashell can be sensed from its shape and texture as man holds it in his hand, from the pulsing echo of life—of the life of the sea itself—as he puts it to his ear.

The seashell, said Wright, "is a beautiful form of *principle at work*. Every single seashell comes to a different conclusion, wherever it may start or whatever the harmony may be. Shall we call each a different *idea*? . . . No, they are not different. They are all the experience of but *one* idea. Out of that one idea . . . comes infinite variety. Now, is there a *mind*, would you say, producing these infinite changes of form in nature? What is doing this? Science can investigate it but science comes against a barrier it can never pierce. What this inner life is, we do not know. But this innate source of expression is what should inspire you all, give you faith in your own divinity, if that is the word for it, in your own inspiration . . . You see," Wright said, "there never is a limit. Nothing in nature indicates that the variety could end, so long as the principle is inviolate. . . ."

On Wednesday, the 21st of October, 1959, the Solomon R. Guggenheim Museum was officially opened to the millions of New York city dwellers, visitors, and tourists who for the past three years had watched this strange, unlikely building mushroom its way upwards and outwards from the confining reaches of its sober Fifth Avenue neighbors. The official ceremonies took place at noon. The Mayor of New York was there, the United States Ambassador to the United Nations, the Secretary of Health, Education and Welfare, museum presidents, park and city officials. The President of the United States sent a letter to be read. Many speeches were made before the white ribbon was finally cut and the mass of people who had stood in silence watching on the street began their slow procession into the building. Inside, they found a domed and spiralled space, a great ramp circling the interior like the ribs of the seashell to rise gently to the sun-flooded dome above.

Olgivanna Wright, Mrs. Frank Lloyd Wright, tall, handsome, poised, her dark hair streaked with gray, was also there that day. For Olgivanna Wright the ceremonies marked more than the opening of a museum. They marked the celebration of the years of her marriage to a man who had never ceased to grow, to learn; who had never ceased to wonder at the miracle of life; who had never ceased to give whatever he had to it; who had never ceased to enjoy whatever life had to give to him. For Olgivanna Wright the ceremonies also marked, she knew, the first of many such occasions when she would stand alone in public receiving honors in her husband's name, when she would be faced with the varied and difficult decisions in the carrying on of the work at Taliesin, when she would need courage and spirit, vigor and faith.

Frank Lloyd Wright was not there that day. He was dead. On April 9th, 1959, Frank Lloyd Wright, almost 90 years old, died. He died in the hour just before dawn. He might almost have planned it that way. His worktable at

[*183*]

"This eleventh-hour building is a thoroughbred."

Guggenheim Museum, New York, 1959

Louis Reens

"Mr. Guggenheim . . . didn't want just another museum."

Guggenheim Museum interior, across the ramps

Louis Reens

". . . it is all one thing, all an integral, not part put to part."

Guggenheim Museum, looking down

Louis Reens

"You will never lose the sense of sky."

Guggenheim Museum, skylight

Louis Reens

Taliesin West was piled with projects and drawings of buildings still to come. The Guggenheim Museum was nearing completion. Architects from Taliesin were engaged in buildings, large and small, across the country.

Frank Lloyd Wright had received just about every honor, national and international, a man could want:—from the Gold Medal of the Royal Institute of British Architects to the Gold Medal Award of his lifelong enemy, the American Institute of Architects. He had been an invited and honored visitor to many countries and many continents. His work had been shown in museums and travelling art exhibits in many places. His work had been published both at home and abroad. He now had honorary degrees to place after his name, if he wanted to, bestowed on him by several ranking universities. Well, he had got along pretty well for a good many years without all these official signs of public acknowledgment, he thought wryly. Just the same, recognition was good. So was fame. Or was it, he wondered with a flash of his well known caustic wit, only notoriety, after all? Whatever it was, it wasn't really what counted. What counted was—yes, what he had done. Do it! Build it! Be it! That was what counted.

The hour before dawn! How much he had accomplished in that hour in his lifetime. In the sanctum sanctorum of the cottage overlooking the changing waters of Lake Mendota; in the Oak Park Studio with the birds beginning to greet the morning in the willow tree beyond his window; in the old Imperial Annex, with the fire in the hearth fallen to ashes; in Taliesin, with the sky growing pink in the mirror of the courtyard pool.

"An hour when all is still and I am rested," wrote Frank Lloyd Wright. "An hour when I know I can turn over and rest several hours more: then things come clearest; then problems seem to work themselves out with little help from me. . . . "

At a quarter to five on that April morning, 1959, Frank Lloyd Wright, recovering from an operation six days earlier, turned over to rest a little more; turned over; sighed; and, as though he had added "tired to tired" one too many times, he died.

He lies buried in the graveyard of his Lloyd-Jones ancestors, in the beloved Wisconsin Valley—just beyond the weatherbeaten walls of the chapel in the woods where, as a boy, he sat Sunday after Sunday in a rocking chair and listened to the readings from the Book, and to the words of his preacher aunts and uncles. He listened, and long years afterward, he remembered:

"The time of Grace has come.

Freely we have received.

Freely then, let us give.

Grace? The gift of freedom to the strong soul.

The time of Grace has come: yes, the time of Grace to
   others.

Live up to life—Man loves Beauty.

So it is, that Beauty loves Man."

Many people—architects, writers, artists, and historians —have tried in one way or another to sum up the life and work of Frank Lloyd Wright. Wright tried, too, in books and articles, in speeches and interviews. He was in his way a philosopher, and a poet with words as well as with buildings, as a look into the pages of his own *Autobiography* will quickly bear out.

Poetry, imagination, wit; a firm belief in first principles, in the dignity of man and the reality of Nature; intuition and the knowledge that enabled him to make use of it, these were all his. They made his buildings architecture.

Also his was the kind of sense of humor that turned up unexpectedly now and then. It was a saving grace when the going got too hard, the discussion too ponderous. It confounded the intellectual more than once, but it delighted the listener; and it gave Wright a chance to say in another way to both admirer and critic what he had been saying all his life: that he was simply, after all, a man. Not a saint or a god or a devil, but an artist and a man. Which was quite enough for him and should, he thought, be enough for anybody.

"In your long life of practical and artistic endeavor," asked an informed and earnest interviewer before a national television audience, "what do you consider your most satisfactory achievement, Mr. Wright?"

"Oh, my dear boy," Mr. Wright answered, "the next one, of course!"

Thereby he summed it all up, as well if not better than anyone else has ever been able to do for him.

ACKNOWLEDGEMENTS

My personal gratitude for the graciousness and encouragement of Maginel Wright Barney; and for the guidance of my friend, Frank d'Autilia, architectural troubleshooter for this book.

Doris Ransohoff

Our thanks to Olgivanna Lloyd Wright and Iovanna Wright for their critical advice; and to Eugene Masselink, Secretary to the Frank Lloyd Wright Foundation, and his colleagues for help in procuring photographs and their interested encouragement.

The Editors